HAUNTED COCHISE COUNTY

FRANCINE POWERS

Haunted America

Published by Haunted America
A Division of The History Press
Charleston, SC
www.historypress.com

Cover images are from author's collection.

First published 2023

Manufactured in the United States

ISBN 9781467151894

Library of Congress Control Number: 2022948297

Notice: The information in this book is true and complete to the best of our knowledge. It is offered without guarantee on the part of the author or The History Press. The author and The History Press disclaim all liability in connection with the use of this book.

I dedicate this book to the family members we lost in a span of five months. My dad, Matias; my sister Stella; my grandson Baby Michael; and my cousin Freddy. In gratitude to my family, who shared the same insufferable losses and for their support and time on the journey to write this book.

CONTENTS

Preface   7
Introduction   9

Crook Tunnel   17
Bisbee   22
Tombstone   66
Douglas   113
Horseshoe Café   129
Carr House   143
The Cochise Hotel   149
Camp Naco   153

Bibliography   157
About the Author   160

PREFACE

I'm a third-generation Bisbee and Cochise County native. My maternal grandfather was born in Bisbee in 1904 and was a laborer for the mining companies. My father, Matias V. Rojas, was a dump truck driver at the Lavender Pit and worked his way up to work underground as a driller.

I'm an Arizona Foundation Newspaper award-winning reporter. I authored the first book about ghosts in Bisbee, called *Mi Reina: Don't Be Afraid*, and I'm the author of *Haunted Bisbee*, which has been adapted to a children's book called *Ghostly Tales of Bisbee*.

I've been collecting Bisbee history, paranormal and not, since high school and really became serious about it in my twenties. I have been on many different television shows, including *Ghost Hunters*, for which I did an interview at the Copper Queen Hotel in 2006. I also published an online magazine called *Spirits of Cochise County* that covered paranormal activity in the surrounding areas, including old ghost stories plus the several I have originated and are still being used today.

I had my first experience with ghosts at the age of six in my childhood home in Bisbee. I penned explicit details regarding the experiences there and the many more I've had throughout my life. Those supernatural encounters opened me up to having the gift of mediumship.

I was the owner-operator of Bisbee Historical Haunted Tours from 2013 to 2016, until I relocated to Tucson. I'm also a member of the Cochise County Historical Society.

My own family history revolves around two separate connections to the Mexican Revolution that changed the life paths of my paternal grandparents. Although they became American citizens in the 1940s and owned a successful business in Douglas, their childhood was difficult. My great-grandmother was shot and killed by a stray bullet during a battle when my grandmother was a ten-year-old girl. This death left my grandmother and her brother orphaned. Soon after, they were sent to live with an aunt in Douglas.

When my grandfather was thirteen, my great-grandmother saved him from the clutches of Pancho Villa. Villa had ridden through their village, looking for supplies and more men and children to serve as "water boys" for his army. She was able to find a way to hide my grandfather, saving him from becoming a prisoner of war. When my grand-uncle, the older brother of my grandfather, was twenty-three, he rode with Pancho Villa and was a "Villista."

Although I grew up hearing about this situation from my now deceased father, Matias, his younger sister, my Aunt Jenny, has documented more family history. Their uncle rode with Villa to the town of Aqua Prieta, Sonora, and was involved in what is known as the Aqua Prieta Battle. My ancestor was wounded by a sword during the fight but recovered and traveled back to Douglas in 1920, where my father's family ultimately settled.

Cochise County has been my home to both sides of my family for more than one hundred years. It's of the utmost importance to maintain the historical aspect of researching the paranormal in the area. It's in my family lineage to pay respect to the people who have lived and died in Cochise County, the only place I know as home.

Finally, I have to specially thank the Cochise County Archives and Kevin Pyles for all of their help with this project.

INTRODUCTION

In Cochise County, the history of America's Wild West stays etched in its mountains, rivers and deserts. Its lovely scenery of robust sunsets—with glorious layers of different oranges, reds, purples and luminous yellows—is legendary. Its landscape is blanketed with an array of cacti, mesquite, red clay soil and magnificent mountain ranges.

Cochise County was created on February 1, 1881, and was named for Cochise, a Cho-ken (Chiricahua) Apache chief. Its area is a total of 6,219 square miles, and it has a current approximate population of about 132,000 people. It is in the most southeastern corner of Arizona and borders the state of Sonora, Mexico. The existence of the county was made possible due to the Gadsden Purchase of 1853, permitting additions of land to the United States.

This accumulation of land included the New Mexico Territory, and on February 24, 1863, President Abraham Lincoln signed the Organic Act, creating the Arizona Territory. It was directed that the part of the territory of New Mexico that runs west of a line running due south would be designated as the Arizona Territory. Four years later, officers, including a governor and a territorial delegate, were elected. The new territory was divided into four counties, including Pima County, with Tucson being its county seat. In 1881, Cochise County was separated from Pima County, with Tombstone being made its county seat. Arizona became a state on February 14, 1912.

The area where Cochise County is located saw native people flourishing for thousands of years. Countless archaeological digs have uncovered many

The United States commemorated Francisco Vásquez de Coronado's expedition by establishing the Coronado National Memorial outside Sierra Vista, Arizona, in 1952. *Author's collection.*

cultural sites that shows civilizations, some even from the Stone Age. These findings calculate that civilizations existed in the area ten to twelve thousand years ago. Many generations of people native to the continent thrived here, long before the Europeans arrived. There were different tribes and nations within the land, and people were either living in harmony or at war. The native people fought over territory, food supplies and everything in between. According to history documents, Spaniards arrived here about eighty years before the Pilgrims landed on Plymouth Rock.

After Europeans landed in North America, they made a trek across the continent to make territorial claims and take advantage of the vast supply of game, land and the rich soil for farming. Christopher Columbus, who served under the Spanish Crown, was the explorer who introduced North America to Spain. This, in turn, inspired the Crown to maintain a powerful grip on the region, particularly in Cochise County and Mexico.

Captain General Francisco Vásquez de Coronado began a two-year journey in 1540 from Compostela, Mexico, to locate and claim the fabled cities of Cibola, or the Seven Cities of Gold, through what is now southeastern Arizona. He and his large exploration party consisting of cavalrymen and foot soldiers came across the San Pedro River Valley, and the mission ended in failure.

After the Spanish arrived in this region, Native Americans came together to fight against European rule. Some of the tribes more infamous for their retaliation include the Yaquis and Apaches. The Spaniards and Mexicans had the roughest time keeping the Apache tribes at bay for lengthy periods of time.

Northern areas of Mexico, such as the state of Sonora, were left unprotected during the wars of independence between 1810 and 1823. Some of this area is now part of southern Arizona.

Eventually, by 1830, Mexico had gained independence from Spain, but it continued to war against the Apaches. The Mexican government did not intercede, leaving its citizens to fend for themselves. In turn, citizens hired individuals to shield themselves from the six different Apache tribes.

The Mexican state of Sonora finally intervened in 1835 and instituted a grotesque, savage program. The governor of Sonora placed an order for men to hunt down Apaches and be rewarded for their actions. Payment would be made only with a trade of an Apache scalp—for a male over the age of fourteen, it was one hundred pesos; for women, they would pay fifty; and for children, twenty-five pesos were paid.

This led to an ongoing war of brutal acts of revenge between the Mexicans and the Chiricahuas, resulting in a large number of deaths for decades. Both sides of the conflict saw equal acts of tortures, ambushes, kidnapping and massacres, including of women and children. As every chief from the sub-tribes of the Apache Nation began to die off, their revulsion for the Mexicans grew even stronger. Chief Cochise was one of those who carried that hatred with him all the way to his grave.

Cochise (1804–1874) lived in the Dragoon and Chiricahua Mountains and led violent raiding parties on either side of those areas and into northern Mexico. He was considered to be a very brave warrior and a leader of uncommon intelligence.

After some time, Cochise realized that he couldn't continue to fight Mexicans and the United States at the same time. He chose to make treaties with the United States, as his animosity for Mexicans overpowered his feelings for the Anglos.

Two years after his decision to attempt a sort of reconciliation with the United States, an agreement for the Chiricahua Apache Indian Reservation was dissolved by President Ulysses S. Grant. This was not an official settlement, but rather one that depended on an honest handshake between himself and General Oliver Howard made in 1872. The reservation that the Apache chief agreed on went from the border of the Arizona Territory and Mexico and then up above Fort Bowie around to the Dragoon Springs and the Cochise Stronghold—a place that Cochise believed would be safe. This action taken by the government resulted in more retaliation and revenge on the United States as part of the Apache War effort.

In the range of the Chiricahua Mountains, as seen from Rhyolite Park, there is a very curious silhouette that looks like a man lying down. You can easily see a profile of a head and shoulders. This site is called "Cochise's Head."

Geronimo was another legendary Apache leader. The Mexicans began to call him that directly after the massacre of Kaskiyeh. He was born in June 1829 and belonged to one of the six sub-tribes of the Apache people called the Bedonkohe. This gruesome event took place in the summer of 1858 as the result of another massacre that included Geronimo's entire family. His mother, wife and children were all slaughtered during a trading trip. His tribe were camped outside the Mexican town the Apaches called Kaskiyeh. This is where Mexican troops killed his family and murdered all the warriors guarding the campsite. They likewise killed many other women and children, stole their horses and weapons and destroyed their supplies.

Geronimo was the fourth child of a family of four boys and four girls. He was born and raised in an area called No-doyohn Canon, Arizona. This is now in the area of modern-day Clifton, Arizona. He was born with the name Goyahkla, which translates to "The One Who Yawns." He was raised as a farmer but ultimately became a shaman. Although he was considered a holy man and healer, he became one of the most dangerous warriors of his time.

Geronimo continued fighting with Mexico and with the United States until he was sequestered in March 1886 after a long and relentless pursuit led by General George Crook. Upon his capture, his only request was that his people, after submitting to imprisonment, would be allowed to return to the Arizona Territory. Sadly, this never came to be, and the Chiricahuas were sent to Florida. Geronimo instead escaped to Mexico along with some of his group, and within only a few months, in Skeleton Canyon, he finally surrendered to the U.S. Cavalry and to General Nelson Miles. By 1894, he had been sent to Fort Sill, Oklahoma, and died on February 17, 1909.

Cochise County has an incredible history and connection to Mexico and the Apache Wars, and it has over the years overcome its tragedies. The "Five Cs" of Arizona stand for cattle, cotton, climate, copper and citrus. These are very relevant to the county's story and accomplishments.

Cochise County is home to many ranches with a variety of cattle breeds; in later years, guest ranches would thrive here. The mile-high community of Bisbee was home to one of the most successful copper mines in the world at one time. Copper is the main reason why Douglas, another county city, was created. Other minerals have been excavated and made Cochise County a "boom" area.

Cochise County holds a few fantastic facts to its credit. Near the town of Sierra Vista and at the San Pedro River, there is the greatest variety of hummingbirds in the world. The county has had success with cotton farms and cattle and, of course, mining. There are astonishing true stories of stagecoach and train robberies, along with other nefarious events involving Wyatt Earp and the Cochise County Cowboys. The United States built famous army forts here, including Fort Bowie, Fort Huachuca and Camp Naco.

Goyahkla, who the Mexicans called "Geronimo," was once a holy man but is remembered as one of the most ruthless warriors in history. *Author's collection.*

Ore wagons with twenty-plus mule teams ready to deliver tons of ore to various mining smelters across early Cochise County. *Author's collection.*

A stagecoach driver is seen in a ghostly reflection of a window in Tombstone. *Jonathon Donahue.*

Scorpions, centipedes, vinegaroons and diamondback rattlesnakes all live in Cochise County, along with pumas (mountain lions), black bears, bobcats, coyotes and javelina.

Cochise County has been a popular backdrop for Hollywood movies, videos and television shows, as well as media that tell its stories, which stretch over the more than 140 years it has been in existence. Its landscape can't be replicated, and its past can't be forgotten as part of America's history, good and bad. It has an enjoyable climate that feels perfect for hiking and biking on its many trails across the region. At night, the stars glow bright and set the scene for special adventures, and during the day, indescribable blue skies umbrella the desert. There are numerous wineries, breweries and one-of-a-kind shops and galleries to visit. Cochise County's history is poetic. It's like living in a western paradise.

CROOK TUNNEL

THE HOODOO

There is a type of superstition that has sat solid with mining and railroad personnel for many years. Crook Tunnel has publicly been named by railroad men to be part of the "Hoodoo" of the number three—as in bad luck comes in threes. There were three severe accidents in or very near the tunnel and seemed to set off a sort of curse on that length of railroad track. Maybe the workers were on to something. This tunnel had a lot of problems from the word go and seemed to continue throughout its history.

Crook Tunnel is situated east of Gold Gulch and four miles west of Bisbee Junction. This was the El Paso and Southwestern Bisbee train tunnel. The AZ & Southwestern railway built a sixty-mile railroad from Benson south to Bisbee in the late 1880s. The railway at the time went through the towns of Curtis, Fairbanks, Hereford and then to Bisbee Junction. The railroad was eventually sold to El Paso and Southwestern. In 1902, they extended the railroad to El Paso to the town of Douglas in Arizona. This is when Crook Tunnel was constructed. Eventually, this section of railroad was abandoned, as was the tunnel.

Cement work to cover the walls and inner ceiling of Crook Tunnel was done in 1905. Rock had to be removed before the cementing work began, and it took about thirty days to finish. There was a lot of falling rocks, and this was the best solution for that problem at the time.

Crook Tunnel and the Hoodoo curse. *Debe Branning.*

In June of the same year, because of a cave-in at Crook Tunnel, the Calumet and Arizona Mining Company had to stop underground work. Miners were laid off, and ore bins stayed full due to the blockade, which lasted for two days. The cave-in happened at the end of the tunnel due to a new cut in the mountain, where beams had been run in eighty feet.

Work had been done behind the timber and was about to be removed when the retaining walls outside the tunnel fell, causing an avalanche of dirt and of debris.

During the winter of 1909, on December 3, twelve train cars went into a ditch near Crook Tunnel. A full ore train heading to Bisbee wrecked because of spreading rails, according to the *Bisbee Daily Review*. This blocked traffic for an entire day.

Let's get to the beginning of the curse of the "Hoodoo" that the workers believed was attached to the tunnel. On February 22, 1908, on a sharp curve of the railroad right before and south of Crook Tunnel, forty-eight-year-old widower Fred John was riding his motorcycle fitted to the rails and hit a heavy ore train from Bisbee—head on. John was heading toward Bisbee at a high speed, and at the curve in the road he must have heard the whistle of the train coming in the other direction but was going too fast and couldn't stop in time or maneuver himself in any way.

He was thrown about fifteen feet to the side of the roadbed, while the motorcycle was demolished. The train engineer brought the train to a stop after a short distance and, with another person on the train, ran back and tended to John, who was unconscious. He was taken to the Copper Queen Hospital in Douglas and never regained consciousness. He passed away at six o'clock the same night. His death certificate states that his death was due to a fractured skull. John was a roadmaster for the El Paso & Southwestern railroad and had a son who worked in local railroad shops. They both lived in Douglas. In an eerie coincidence, Ed Scanlon, another roadmaster of the same division near Rodeo, New Mexico, died the same way a few weeks before John's accident. So, to be safe, John took out an accident insurance policy three weeks prior to his own fatal crash.

On April 20, 1912, a brakeman for the El Paso and Southwestern railroad named E.C. Van Wye was knocked off a moving train in Crook's Tunnel by a rock that fell from the roof of the tunnel. As he was braking past the tunnel, the boulder dropped, hitting him on the head and knocking him from the train. His right foot fell across an outer rail of the track when he hit the ground, and then several train cars ran over it. As soon as people realized what had happened, the wounded Van Wye was taken to Bisbee for his injuries. He ended up losing his foot. It was reported by September that he had bought an EMF car (an American car company from 1909 to 1912) with the money he received from the accident.

One of the more graphic and intense incidents in the tunnel was reported in the newspaper the *Coconino Sun*. A badly mangled corpse was discovered in June 1912 by railroad men. The body was lying beside the track in Crook tunnel, soon identified as Henry A. Marks, who was a well-known Bisbee resident from the Warren District. The railroad men found blood on the pilot of the train engine, leading them to search the track. He was known to be staying with Len Christiansen at the time near the tunnel. He had made a trip to Bisbee the day before he was killed.

Witnesses told the county coroner that Marks was drunk when he left Bisbee, and it was assumed that when he got off the train, he had laid down beside or on the track and was struck by another train being brought to Bisbee to be cleaned. Constable Bailey investigated and didn't find any new clues on how the accident occurred. The verdict of the coroner was that the train that ran over Marks had passed through Crook's tunnel between 8:30 p.m. and 9:30 p.m.

The last time anyone saw him Marks was when he was getting off the train at the tunnel at 6:30 p.m. When his body was found, both arms and both legs were broken, and the body looked like it was rolled along the railroad. It was reported that one of his arms was almost completely severed.

At the time of the investigation, it was believed that he was a single man with no relatives. He was taken to the morgue at the O.K. Undertakers in Bisbee. Sadly, it was discovered only after his funeral that he was a married man with children in California. According to the *Bisbee Daily Review*, an investigation to find his family was soon underway. No notation was made when they found his family.

The Hoodoo of Crook Tunnel seemed to go beyond accidents. A bizarre series of deaths related to screw worms had a connection to Crook Tunnel. Four people living in the northern and southern part of the Arizona Territory all fell victim to the maggot-making blowfly. According to an article in the *Arizona Republican*, these insects usually affect livestock and canines—about the only way the blowfly could enter a human is through the nose. The insect is especially partial to blood when laying its eggs. When these eggs hatch, they become known as screw worms. The victim may not realize that he or she has been invaded until it's too late.

One victim, fifty-seven-year-old Elizabeth C. Swan, was the wife of a telegrapher who was assigned to Crook Tunnel. She was reported to have fainted after a severe nosebleed and immediately lay down and slept for a long time. During her sleep, it was supposed, a blowfly had crawled into her nose and laid several eggs. Within hours she had severe pain in her nose, and by the next day, her face had become very swollen. She had unbearable pain and called for a doctor. Upon Dr. O.W. Brandon's examination, he stated that maggots had hatched and eaten a hole the size of a dime in the roof of her mouth!

The doctor sprayed her nose with a dilution of chloroform. He was in a serious conundrum, knowing that the spray was sufficient to kill the worms, but it would probably do the same to Swan. About nine days after the operation, she died. She was said to be in unbelievable agony at her home in Osborne and passed away at three o'clock in the morning on July 20, 1905. Her death certificate states that her cause of death was "exhaustion of screw worms."

It's not a surprise to connect paranormal activity to Crook Tunnel, especially with the several gruesome and traumatizing incidents that occurred there. It's abandoned now and is a trek to reach. As you come around the curve that leads to the tunnel, one may feel an eerie and suspiciously heavy energy. The tunnel itself is very narrow and has a high ceiling, a perfect fit for an old locomotive.

In monsoon season, the tunnel feels very damp, and the crooked edges of the walls are quite cool to the touch. It is very dark inside; at either end of the track, the phrase "the light at the end of the tunnel" fits perfectly.

Some of the ghostly activity that occurs includes cold spots, disembodied voices and even full-bodied apparitions. At night, witnesses have said that they can hear the faint sound of a train coming at one of the entrances, and some have even reported that they have seen a light peering through the tunnel—a light resembling the kind from an antiquated locomotive. Others have, as they walk the tunnel, heard the crunching sound of footsteps following behind them when no one is there.

Visitors to the tunnel have said that they think the ghostly visitations are connected to Marks. This may be true, as he was killed in a very traumatic and horrific way. He may be attached to the site and is still wandering its track looking for his way out and the way to his family.

The Hoodoo of Crook Tunnel may still be attached, so the next time you head out to explore it, be aware of its cruelty and take heed as you venture inside its walls and protect yourself from its ancient curse.

BISBEE

One of the most charming towns within the borders of Cochise County is a place set in the most mountainous area of the region, dripping with intriguing history. This place is called Bisbee and is a mining community that was once proudly hailed as the "Queen of Copper Camps"—a company town sculpted by the movement of mountain and rock, backbreaking labor and implausible determination. After the fall of its great mining industry in 1975, it has been reinvented as an artist community.

Originally, the area was in Pima County and called the Southern Dragoon Mountains. In 1877, deep into these mountains, U.S. Army lieutenant John A. Rucker with fifteen men of Company C, Sixth Cavalry, from Fort Bowie, along with John (Jack) Dunn, arrived. They were on an expedition to see if members of the Chiricahua Apache tribe had an encampment in the area.

After Lieutenant Rucker and his group camped overnight, Dunn went on a mission to find good drinking water. He found a fresh spring flowing over what is now called Castle Rock and found an indication of the presence of lead, copper and silver. Soon after, Rucker, Dunn and their packer, T.D. Byrne, claimed the first mine there and called it the Rucker.

A few weeks later, a prospector with a long life of trauma and drama named Gorge Warren was grubstaked by Dunn to find more rich spots in the area. Warren was supposed to name Dunn in all notices of places he might find. Warren found more claims but never listed Dunn on any of the several he located.

What once was a mining giant is now an artist community. *Author's collection.*

Only fifty-six days after the Rucker Mine was discovered, Warren found a second mining claim in the area, naming it the Mercy Mine. He is considered by some to be the "Father of Bisbee."

Years later, Warren gambled several claims in a footrace against a horse in Charleston, Arizona. He lost that race and eventually all his remaining claims to deceitful and greedy business partners. In the last years of his life, he worked at different saloons sweeping the floors and cleaning the spittoons.

The mines and surrounding properties were solely owned in later years by the Phelps Dodge Company but are now owned by Freeport McMoRan Copper and Gold.

The name of the booming mining camp was given in honor of Judge DeWitt Bisbee, of the brokerage firm of Williams and Bisbee of San Francisco. He loaned $20,000 to the engineering firm of Martin and Ballard to buy the Copper Queen prospect.

The C&A Mining Company decided that the nationally acclaimed City Beautiful movement would be an excellent model for the new town site of Warren. It was completed around 1907. Other notable areas that sprang up in later Bisbee history include San Jose, Bakerville, Briggs, Don Luis, Galena, Tintown and Saginaw.

Top: A Bisbee mural by the late artist Rose Johnson depicts Bisbee's history impeccably. *Jenny Chavez.*

Bottom: OK Street in Bisbee showcasing the Pythian Castle and the town's splendor and distinctiveness. *Author's collection.*

Bisbee was founded in 1880 and incorporated in 1902. In 1929, the county seat was changed from Tombstone to Bisbee. There are 2,300 miles of mine tunnels under Bisbee, Lowell and Warren. During Bisbee's mining period, more than 3 million ounces of gold and 8 billion pounds of copper were extricated. Elevation is 5,300 feet. The original segment of Bisbee and its residential area became a historical district in 1980.

BISBEE'S CITY PARK

An extraordinary concrete park sits in an area on Brewery Avenue and below a street named Opera Drive in the heart of Brewery Gulch, an area of old town in Bisbee. As it basks in the sun and offers a place for various entertainments, such as a playground for the children and a stage for concerts, it was also surprisingly Bisbee's first city cemetery. The pioneer graveyard was created sometime in the late 1880s. The cemetery had become so neglected and run-down that it was closed and brilliantly converted into the town park. Another idea why the cemetery was shut down was that it was a public health concern. As the burial ground was upslope from water wells, the water would be contaminated, causing or adding to the typhoid outbreaks taking place in the town's early history.

A collage of photos in the *Bisbee Review* dated February 2, 1913, shows laundry being dried on some of the fences surrounding the graves of the dead. Tombstones were falling apart and in shambles. Maybe the grave sites were in that condition because there wasn't family left in Bisbee to tend to them. The majority of those buried there were single men, with some from other countries without families nearby. The site was also an embarrassment and a danger to neighborhood children.

As early as 1910, complaints were brought to the city council as residents sought a solution. Plans were eventually brought to the council, but the board and Bisbee residents chose to use the property for a playground instead. Children were already using the old cemetery as a play area anyway. If they weren't there, they were running in the very narrow streets, barely avoiding cars, horses and wagons—a chaotic and unsafe situation.

According to an announcement made in the *Bisbee Daily Review* in March 1913, a playground committee was formed by the Warren District Commercial Club to plan for a park for the neighborhood children. Another *Bisbee Daily Review* article, "Dilapidated Graveyard or Playground, Which?," reported

The site of Bisbee's first cemetery. *Author's collection.*

that members of the committee, during a council meeting, explained the law regarding city and town cemeteries enacted by the legislative assembly of the territory of Arizona. The law reads that whenever any ground used as a cemetery within any city limits has been abandoned and ceases to be used for such purposes to better advantage, the city or town can use the grounds. The remains of the persons buried there can be removed to a cemetery or another suitable place. The expense of such removal is to be paid by the city or town.

The law also reads that whenever the remains are removed, all monuments and gravestones shall also be removed and replaced at the new cemetery. The graves were to be numbered and a list of the names of the buried kept. The decision of abandoning of the old cemetery was made easily. During a special meeting with the city council in January 1913, Secretary J.H. Gray of the commercial club said, "We want to place all of these bodies where they will be decently cared for, where the graves will be kept as they should be. We want no desecration of graves but on the contrary, want them made sacred."

Money was raised to renovate the neglected monstrosity, to move the bodies buried in the pioneer burial ground to a new site in Lowell called Evergreen Cemetery and to buy playground equipment.

On April 25, 1913, one of the most despicable events took place at the old cemetery. The *Bisbee Daily Review* ran this incredible headline on April 26: "Brought Head from Battle—Gruesome Souvenir of Naco Engagement Found in the Street Yesterday—Interred by Authorities." The article reported that Chief of Police Bassett Watkins received a frantic call to rush to the old cemetery up Brewery Gulch. He dropped everything he was doing. As soon as he arrived, he noticed a crowd of people standing in a circle. He was told nothing about what he was about to see. He pushed his way through, and shockingly, he saw a human head lying on the ground! The head, already in a bad stage of decomposition, was a revolting sight.

After some investigating, it was discovered that individuals had brought up the head from Naco. Their intention was to leave it in a saloon nearby as a souvenir for all to admire. The owner of the saloon refused to have it on the premises and had it taken to the cemetery. It was placed in a shallow grave, and unfortunately, it was dug up by a dog. That same day, the chief had the disembodied head placed in a much deeper hole in the cemetery. This time, a pile of rocks was placed over it so it wouldn't be disturbed again.

The removal of bodies to Evergreen Cemetery began around January 19, 1915, and was completed on January 22. The Palace and Undertaking Company had the contract to clear the cemetery. There were badly organized records of the dead, written only in pencil on various pieces of paper. Many of the names were labeled "unknown," including for a baby. John Tappiner was listed as twenty-five years old when he was killed during the Bisbee Massacre and was listed to be in Grave 3. S.8 E.G.

Some were nervous that not all the bodies were removed, but there was a diplomatic and vigilant transfer of the graves to Evergreen Cemetery before the construction and landscaping of the park began. Of the thirty-four bodies removed and relocated, twenty-three were identified. The last recorded person to be buried there was in 1898, the infant son of H.M. Woods. The city park had a formal dedication on May 20, 1916, with Governor Hunt in attendance.

When I was junior high student, my family moved into the Brewery Gulch neighborhood and lived in a house directly above the city park. At the entrance off the seventy-five steps on the street-free side of the park, I met up with a ghost, a boy. In my book *Mi Reina: Don't Be Afraid*, I journaled about the experience.

I often entered the park through that same entrance, and that is where we would often bump heads. He wasn't evil and gave me a feeling of despair rather than danger. I saw an apparition of the boy several times.

Bisbee's city park today. *Author's collection.*

I saw flashes of a young male pointing, showing me his mother's grave. We know that there are no body-filled coffins under city park, but I do remember feeling that he was a very domineering person. I also felt that he was protecting or watching over something nearby or at the entrance. I saw him pointing at the ground and telling me, *This is hallowed ground and not a place for children to play.*

Meanwhile, in 2004, Debe Branning held a ghost workshop in town and visited the park. We were friends and shared our paranormal enthusiasm.

Branning realized after she read my book that she had a paranormal experience at the same area. She said that while speaking at the same entrance, she suddenly felt a cold, spine-tingling breeze rush through her. She then felt nauseous and dizzy. Days later, whenever she looked into a mirror, a young boy would somehow shadow her own reflection. Later, when she read about my experience at the same site, we, along with Sheila Bontreger, got together and went back.

We stood at the park entrance. Branning asked me to stand where I sensed the boy. I did. She said that was the same spot she had her experience. She grabbed a long twig and put it on the ground. We asked the boy a list of questions and asked that he respond by moving the twig. She videotaped the séance.

He was asked if he remembered me. His response was "Yes." We asked his age. We listed the numbers from nine to fourteen. The twig moved at twelve. We asked if his mother had been buried there. He answered "Yes." We asked if she was still buried there. He answered "Yes." We asked if he was protecting her. He answered "Yes." We asked if he wanted to leave. He said "No."

After a while, he stopped responding. He seemed to vanish or simply grew too tired to communicate. The spirit most likely does not realize that his mother's body was removed and still haunts the site were her grave used to be.

The city park was another stop on my haunted and historical tours, and I had many more paranormal experiences there. Once during a tour, as I was speaking, the large bow on my jacket was untied in front of my guests by invisible hands! On several occasions, I have seen a figure in my peripheral view when no one was standing there. As soon as I am on that site, the ghost rushes to my side. Since Branning had the experience of the boy ghost following her home, I insist that he does not have permission to follow me. I also encouraged guests of all my tours to tell him the same out loud.

The set of stairs and entrance to Bisbee's city park, where Francine Powers has had continuous contact with the ghost of a boy for more than forty years. *Author's collection.*

Other tour guests have recorded a male voice at the same spot and pictures of a white flowy fog in broad sunny daylight. The entrance is not the only place where paranormal activity has been reported. A guest refused to walk near a far tree by the street gate, as she saw a tall person standing still there, watching and listening to the tour. She said it was an unnatural being and couldn't decipher if it was a ghost or demon. This frightened her so much that we had to cut the tour short and leave.

Joey Bravo is the tour guide for the Haunted Bisbee Tours, which is owned by Zandra Bravo. Joey told me that during one of his haunted tours, a little girl was part of the group. He said that there was a ghost box being used by one of his guests. The small child began to communicate with the ghost through the device. She asked if the ghost wanted to play, and it responded with "Hopscotch." The conversation went on for some time, amusing and/or terrifying the people who were witness to the supernatural event.

BISBEE FIRE STATION No. 2

A narrow building with a red garage door holds a story of tragedy honoring the valor of a firefighter who lived to save lives. The very place he worked, Bisbee Fire Station No. 2, is located about in the middle of Tombstone Canyon Road in Bisbee. More than one thousand homes sprang up in the new and expanding neighborhood in Upper Tombstone Canyon, and by 1910, it was one of the swankier parts of town. Citizens were demanding their own fire station by 1914. Surprisingly, some members of the city council were opposed to another fire house, saying that there was not enough fresh water or drainage and that the property was flood-prone. Eventually, the council voted to buy the property for the new fire station. The building was completed on September 30, 1914, and was modernized in 1993.

The plans for the building included a two-story structure, all concrete, with living quarters for the firemen upstairs and a pole for a fast slide down to the main floor, where the horses and wagons were kept.

Bisbee's fire department history includes the first volunteer fire department, which was created on October 1, 1894. The headquarters was located on Main Street, across from where 37 and 35 Main Street sits now. In 1898, a brick structure was built on the north side of the same street as the new headquarters. A bell on top of the building sounded the alert in the case of fires. It was located next to where the Western Bank building is today. The volunteer crew depended on a natural water supply and bucket brigade.

In later years, there was also a fire house located down on Naco Road, near the entrance of what is now Old Bisbee. But the route from there to upper Tombstone Canyon was very curvy for horse-drawn fire wagons, used at that time, and the location didn't sit well for the residents up the canyon.

In May 2008, the Bisbee Fire Department celebrated one hundred years as Arizona's first full-time paid crews. On October 14, 1908, a fire started there that ended up being the most epic fire in Bisbee's history. The fire spread through most of the business district on Main Street, and according to the *Bisbee Daily Review* article "Bisbee Has Three-Quarters Million Fire Loss," published the following day, if a water hose had been available, the fire would've been extinguished within a few minutes.

According to the newspaper, the fire started at 6:10 p.m. in the Grand Hotel, located on the corner of Subway and Main Streets, and raged for three hours. The blaze started in a closet of the hotel and was first seen by Sam Frankenburg from the Fair store and a man named Tommy Blair. The men told the newspaper that with a simple hose, they would've been able to

Bisbee Fire Station No. 2 circa 1914. *Author's collection.*

stop the fire, which destroyed the hotel before traveling down Main Street and then up to Clawson Hill, leaving only two houses standing.

After the fire devoured the Grand Hotel, it headed down the road, hurled across Subway Street and caught the Fair building on fire. Then it spread to the Johnson-Henninger building, better known as the Woolworth building. This structure became a fire wall, stopping the blaze from traveling farther down Main Street. The flames were so high and wide that the Anguis Block building across the street was set on fire. Luckily, a side wall of that structure blocked the brutal flames from feeding off anymore buildings farther east.

Acting like a living creature, the fire turned itself around to spread toward upper Main Street and to a part of the residential district on Clawson Hill. Since this was a mining community and dynamite was easily available, it was used to blow up some buildings near Castle Rock to cause a firebreak. It worked, but the fire caused $750,000 worth of damage in the business section of the town, and $3,000 worth of residential property was destroyed. This was the largest fire ever recorded there.

Let's return to Fire Station No. 2. As you enter the front door, you come into the garage. The first things you see are a fire truck and emergency vehicle. There is also the original fire pole still intact to your left. Before the renovation, the entire upstairs living quarters were completely switched around. The sleeping area was in the front and open with beds lined in rows. The kitchen and recreation area were in the back.

There are two firefighters assigned to each three-day shift at No. 2. The modernization of the building was designed for more people in the future and other crews during other emergency situations, such as wildfire crews. There is a "firehose dryer" in front of the building—the only one of its kind. It is in front of the building and over a nearly fifteen-foot-deep ditch. In the early 1970s, firemen built the structure.

For several years, a rumor circulated around Bisbee that Fire Station No. 2 was haunted. I used to be the editor-in-chief of our family-owned online paranormal magazine called *Spirits of Cochise County*. I organized a ghost hunt to see if the rumor was true. Our ghost hunt, the first at the station, took place in 2009. Members of Spirits of Cochise County Investigators (SCCI) tackled that story.

A former firefighter who had died of a mysterious gunshot wound while at home is the resident ghost. At first, he was thought to have committed suicide, but later, according to interviews with retired Bisbee firefighters, the case was changed to an accidental death. The fireman lived close to the

This building is haunted by a former Bisbee firefighter who believes that he is still on shift. *Author's collection.*

station. When he did not show up for work, a coworker went looking for him at his house and found him dead. The now retired firefighter said that he thinks his friend is haunting the historic building, with several activities resembling practical jokes having taken over the years. He told me that the deceased fireman always said that if he died, he would come back and haunt the station.

Generations of firefighters have had numerous paranormal experiences and express them openly. They also use the resident ghost as part of their initiation of the "new guy" on shift. They'll leave the new firefighter alone in the building or assign him or her to lock up on their own.

Some ghostly activity includes doors down the hall to the bedrooms opening after they have been locked at night and the shower in the upstairs quarters of the station turning on by itself. Numerous witnesses have seen wet footprints along the hallway leading away from the bathroom. Pots and pans jangle around on their own. The apparition of a fireman in different areas of the building is often seen. Witnesses say that they have seen an apparition walk straight through a wall near the kitchen.

Footsteps are heard coming up the steep stairs to the second level when nobody is there. Phantasmal sounds of "tinkering around" downstairs at

Two Bisbee firefighters telling guests on Francine Powers' special Halloween tour about the haunting of Fire Station No. 2. *Author's collection.*

the tool bench near the firetrucks are a common occurrence at the station. Firefighters have also reported that they have felt their hands or arms being touched, such as to wake them while they sleep, and the feeling of being held down while they sleep.

For the duration of our paranormal investigation, a few emergency calls blared through the building. When the second call came in, we caught a chilling electronic voice phenomenon (EVP) of an eerie voice responding to a medical emergency call. During the actual radio correspondence, a male voice belonging to emergency personnel asked a female voice if she needs assistance. The female voice responded. Almost instantly, a disembodied voice responds with "Moving."

If this is the voice of a firefighter from days gone by, he seems to still be on duty. He's listening to conversations in the firehouse and hovers over each bed, making sure that his comrades are resting before the next emergency interrupts their sleep.

During a special Halloween Haunted Bisbee tour I gave recently, I made communication with the firefighter ghost. I was speaking outside the building during a cold and still night. There is a fireman's helmet hanging near the front light. As I spoke, one of my guests on the tour mentioned that the hat was swinging. We realized that the ghost was trying to get my attention and was communicating with me.

The firefighter hardhat light cover that was used by the ghost to communicate. *Author's collection.*

I asked him if he was happy that I was back telling his story. The hat swung left to right. I was filled with emotion as I watched the helmet move. As I continued my tour, I saw the helmet began to swing in circles. I told the spirit, "Thank you for letting me know my work here at the fire station is appreciated by a soul so good and brave." It swung even harder and then suddenly just stopped moving completely. That was a brilliant supernatural encounter.

While I was giving a haunted tour another time, a woman was listening to me and decided to try to sit on the pipe-fence of the cement bridge over a deep ditch directly in front of the building. She said that she could not maintain her balance and exclaimed to

The very spot where the ghost of the firehouse saved a woman from falling into the deep ditch. *Author's collection.*

everyone that "someone" grabbed her arm and pushed her off the fence onto solid ground. She said it was the dead fireman. "He saved me from falling down into the ditch! He saved my life!"

BISBEE SUPERIOR COURTHOUSE

A very heated Cochise County election was held on November 19, 1929, and was covered in several different newspapers. It would be mentioned for years to come in various books. The vote was over moving the Cochise County seat from Tombstone to Bisbee. It was decided on that fall day that the seat would be moved to the copper mining town, and by December 1, the Cochise County Board of Supervisors had a location for the new courthouse, which was on Higgins Hill, off Tombstone Canyon Road. Bonds in the amount of $300,000 were approved on February 25, 1930, for the construction of the Pueblo Deco building. It would be for the courts and offices of the county officials, and a jail would also be built on site.

The total cost of the build was $250,000 and was finished by 1931. The architect was Roy Place from Tucson, and the Clinton Campbell Construction Company in Phoenix served as the contractor. A dedication of the building was held on August 3, 1931, by Arizona governor George W.P. Hunt.

The old jail from the Tombstone Courthouse was removed and placed in the new building. The third floor was originally the county jail and included a dormitory for attendants and trustees. Four cell blocks accommodated a total of sixty-five prisoners. The fourth floor held the jail for eight women and four female juveniles. The fifth floor was a jury dormitory. The new county jail was built in 1985 with 160 cells. That jail is located on Highway 80, on the outskirts of Bisbee.

At the turn of the millennium, I was working at the Bisbee Courthouse as a clerk. Within days of starting work there, I experienced odd phenomena. One morning, I was having a conversation with a security guard named Hector. We discussed the many eerie noises and sensations that the building seemed to produce. I told him about hearing footsteps upstairs in the lobby when no one else was around and being completely creeped out when I had to go upstairs and look for court files in the old jail. I said that when I went downstairs for different files, where the sheriff's department used to be located, I saw an apparition of a women dashing right by me.

Cochise County Superior Court, Bisbee Courthouse. *Author's collection.*

He told me about his own experiences and how he heard similar noises during different shifts and how at random times, the courthouse doors would slam shut on their own. He said that other employees confessed to hearing several voices speaking when they came in for work when the building was empty.

The odd noises and creepy voices may be part of a residual haunting—a memory with a thick string lingering from the past attached to a building filled with erupting emotions.

The female entity I saw in the old sheriff's office isn't the only ghost too stubborn to leave the courthouse. This other ghost has been seen by

Judge John Wilson Ross. *Author's collection.*

many and seen well enough to compare him to his picture hanging in the same building. His name is John Wilson Ross. He was born in November 1863 in Berryville, Arkansas, and was the youngest of a family of eight children. He traveled to Flagstaff in 1888 and taught school at Camp Verde. He later began practicing law at Flagstaff, Prescott and Jerome before arriving in Bisbee. He was the first Cochise County superior judge at the new courthouse. He served there from 1931 to 1942, when he was defeated in the 1942 Democratic primary by Frank E. Thomas. He died on June 30, 1945, in Pueblo, Colorado, at the age of eighty-one.

Judge Ross was a very significant and prominent Bisbee resident. He ran as a Republican candidate for the Superior Court judgeship at Tombstone in 1911, but by 1914, he was holding meetings for the Progressive Party at his office, located in the Medigovich Hall building in Bisbee. He was considered one of the leading lawyers in Arizona and was on many committees and councils.

In the spring of 1918, the judge held a well-attended meeting at the city park to organize the circulation of the petitions for nominating the city as a candidate for the courthouse. By November of that year, while working as a Cochise County attorney, he had accepted the position of associate justice of the Supreme Court of Arizona. He was the brother of Henry D. Ross, who at the time was already a member of the state Supreme Court.

Judge John Ross's wife, Lida Norris Ross, was also involved with the community and was a member of Bisbee's social circle. They shared a lovely, brick-veneered home on Shattuck Street in the Warren District. Lida Ross died on January 19, 1923.

The Bisbee Courthouse is a haunting vision of mystical grandeur, sitting above Tombstone Canyon Road. *Author's collection.*

The ghost thought to be the judge is said to show himself in the old jail on the top floors of the courthouse and the judge's chambers, where the smell of a cigar or cigarettes is also sensed. He has also been seen in the second-floor lobby.

During a ghost hunt at the courthouse, fellow paranormal enthusiast Karla Jensen Rothrock and I witnessed some interesting paranormal activity there. I saw the apparition of Judge Ross in the Division 2 courtroom and saw him walk from the judge's bench back to his chambers.

Rothrock; my husband, Randy; another person; and I went to a room in the basement area of the building near the side of the street. It was more of a large closet than a room, but this is where we as a group decided to sit on the floor and try to communicate with a ghost I had seen years before: a woman with a red dress.

I was using a pendulum for the communication instrument. During the séance, we believe I contacted that same ghost. An interesting thing happened: it seemed the ghost was interested in Rothrock. So, I asked the ghost if it would touch Rothrock, if that's who she wanted to communicate with. Only a few moments passed before Rothrock, with eyes closed, said, "She touched me. She touched my forehead." I was looking at her and saw the expression she made when she felt the ghost touch her. It was a breathtaking moment!

Another witness to the judge was a past custodian who reported that as she was mopping at the foot of the stairway in front of the main entrance of the courthouse and facing the doors, she felt as if someone was looking at her. The feeling was so intense that she had to stop mopping and instinctively turned around and looked up to the small mezzanine of the stairway.

A man dressed in a 1940s three-piece suit was staring back down at her. The county worker was taken aback and said that the man had wired glasses. The worker said he had "crazy eyes." The custodian looked down for a moment, and when she looked up toward the steps again, the apparition had vanished.

All these years after his death, Ross's robust and dominating presence is still felt by many who are brought to this place to be held accountable for their actions or to be acquitted of any charges. Nevertheless, Judge John W. Ross will be witness to their fate and will, in his own way, make sure that the beauty and justice of his courthouse are being preserved.

The Greenway Manor

There is a magnificent mansion in Warren that demonstrates Bisbee's wealthy and successful past. This place was the home of John Campbell Greenway but is now called the Greenway Manor and owned by Gretchen Bonaduce. The Greenway home was built in an Arts and Crafts design, with its construction beginning in 1906. It was built by the Calumet and Arizona Mining Company (C&A) to accommodate its general manager and any mining executives or employees. The two-story manor is sitting on a little over two acres, is about ten thousand square feet in area and has ten bedrooms and eleven bathrooms, plus the large main living area. The property also has a carriage house and other structures on its estate. This home was part of the first stage of creating the Warren District of Bisbee.

Lewis W. Powell was the first to live here with his wife and children. As far as the growth and expansion of the copper mining industry, Mr. Powell was a valuable and influential power broker in Arizona. He was born in New Madrid, Missouri, in 1866. While growing up in Missouri, he was educated by private tutors and also attended public schools in St. Louis. He graduated from Washington and Lee University in Lexington, Virginia. Mr. Powell married Alli Moore Jewell, who was from Lexington, Virginia. Alli's father was Major William T. Jewell, who was an officer in the Confederate army.

Mr. Powell was one of the most engaged public frontrunners for civic, industrial or social advancement in the Warren District. The organization of the Warren District County Club is attributed to him, and he was its first president. He was also the vice-president and director of the First National Bank of Douglas. Powell was also very well known in social circles and a member to several fraternities, and he was a thirty-second-degree Mason. Mr. Powell, along with his wife and three children—Ruth, George and Dorothy—as well as a maid, lived there until he resigned as general manager of C&A in 1910. Captain Greenway, who was later called "Colonel," replaced Powell and arrived there the same year.

Greenway was born on July 6, 1872, in Huntsville, Alabama. His life was full of success, gained by a perseverance that followed him in everything he did. He was an 1895 Yale University PhD engineering graduate and renowned quarterback and baseball catcher. He even had an 1894 football card with the advertisement for Mayo Cut Plug tobacco. Right after graduation, for a brief time, he joined the Carnegie Steel Company, located in Duquesne, Pennsylvania.

Above: The Greenway Manor, located in the Warren District of Bisbee, has been defined by mediums and paranormal investigators as a "haunted mansion." *Author's collection.*

Left: John C. Greenway's 1894 Yale football tobacco card. *Wikimedia Commons.*

He was a very close friend with Teddy Roosevelt and joined the ranks of the Rough Riders. He was commissioned in the First Volunteer Cavalry and fought at the Battle of San Juan Hill in 1898 during the Spanish-American War. He received a Silver Star for his efforts in this battle and was originally commissioned as a second lieutenant but was promoted to brevet and then acting captain.

In August 1910, Mr. Greenway's mother, Alice, moved into the company mansion. She was welcomed into the high society of the thriving and growing suburb of Warren. Many years later, Greenway married Isabella Selmes on November 4, 1923; she later became the first woman from Arizona elected to serve in the House of Representatives. Isabella built the Arizona Inn, located in Tucson, with the sale of her copper stock in 1930.

The couple had a son in October 1924 whose nickname was Jack. They lived alternately in Bisbee; Santa Barbara, California; and in Ajo, where Greenway built a home in 1925. Greenway retired his position as general manager of C&A in 1925. Sadly, he died on January 19, 1926, from a blood clot, four days after a gall bladder surgery in New York, at the age of fifty-four. He was buried in Ajo, but his body was disinterred on November 5, 1995, and then reburied in a family vault at the Dinsmore Homestead in Kentucky.

He was said to be tall, dashing and handsome. There is a Gutzon Borglum statue of Greenway at the Polly Rosenbaum Archives and History Building, close to the Arizona capitol. Borglum was one of the artists who created the presidential figures on the Mount Rushmore National Memorial in South Dakota. There is also a Greenway statue created by the same sculptor at the Arizona Historical Society in Tucson, Arizona.

Before Bonaduce bought the mansion, David and Karen Berridge made it their home during the early 2000s. They took three years to restore the house to its original glory. According to the article "The Home as Art" in the *Bisbee Daily Review*, the couple spent an estimated $400,000 on the restoration.

The front door is solid wood and flanked by original stained-glass windows inlaid with copper. The front entry is 480 square feet and features oak-paneled walls. There is a narrow walnut-encased elevator that was added sometime in the 1930s. There are oak wooden floors, and its ceiling has original copper light fittings; the dining room has a hand-painted mural and bookcases made from Douglas fir. Wood paneling also adorns the walls of the 800-square-foot living room.

I was privileged to conduct a ghost hunt and host a formal séance at the historical home and then conduct an interview with the owner of the

Gretchen Bonaduce said about owning the Greenway Manor, "How awesome to be able to live in a house this grand that has so much historical significance to Bisbee." *Sherry Lee.*

Greenway Manor. Gretchen is the mother of two, an American reality TV star who has appeared in *Deadliest Home Video* and *Celebrity Paranormal Project.* She also appeared on the reality show *Breaking Bonaduce* along with her ex-husband of eighteen years, Danny Bonaduce.

Gretchen Bonaduce is additionally a producer and the author of *Surviving Agent Orange: And Other Things I Learned from Being Thrown Under the Partridge Bus.* She is also the lead vocalist of the band the Fatal 80s. Gretchen moved to Bisbee from Los Angeles a few years ago and said, "I think this place found me," while explaining how she came to owning the Greenway Manor.

She told me about her final decision on buying the manor. She said, "I had to go to Phoenix for a book signing so I coincided with that trip to coming to Bisbee and to see the home. I walked through the front door and took one look and said, 'Ok. I'm selling everything to get this house.'"

Gretchen has made the manor into a rock-and-roll Airbnb, with all the rooms following that theme. There is a Beatles room and a Johnny Cash room, an Elvis room, a David Bowie room, a Bob Marley room and a Rolling Stones room. Gretchen has an interest in preserving Bisbee's history and knew that the house was a historical site when she bought it. She said, "How awesome to be able to live in a house this grand that has so much historical significance to Bisbee."

John Greenway supposedly lived on this side of the house, while high-ranking miners would have lived in the several apartments on the other side of the manor. President Roosevelt visited here on different occasions, and it is also thought that in the living room of the manor, the heads of the mining company may have come up with the idea of the Bisbee Deportation of 1917.

The Bisbee Deportation of 1917, a major event for Bisbee miners and residents, took place on July 12, 1917. This event involved the illegal gathering and deportation of more than 12,000 miners who were striking against the C&A and Phelps Dodge mining companies. The Industrial Workers of the World (IWW), or Wobblies, presented a list of demands to the mining companies involved. The mining officials refused those requests, and as a result, the Bisbee Miners Union called a strike on June 24. By June 27, half of the Bisbee workforce was on strike. Armed deputized men gathered and walked about 1,200 strikers to the Warren Ball Park to be loaded into train boxcars and hauled to a government-maintained camp in Columbus, New Mexico. In the end, the mining company was found at fault, as the deportation was wholly illegal and lacked authority in law, either state or federal.

Now, as far as any paranormal activity at the manor goes, Gretchen says that she sometimes feels like Greenway is still in the home. Although she hasn't seen him, she has the feeling that he oversees things in the manor. She stated, "A lot of people who have stayed here have said things to me like, 'My animals don't want to come inside'; they've told me, 'I was awoken suddenly to someone standing over me.'" Gretchen also said footsteps are heard pacing, between two and five o'clock in the morning, upstairs in the hallway.

Gretchen's friend Alison DuBois has come to visit and has picked up on the supernatural energies at the manor. DuBois is an internationally renowned psychic medium and astrologer. There was also a television series called *Medium* that was based on DuBois's life in Phoenix. DuBois told Gretchen what she thinks about the manor: "It's totally haunted and there are tons of miners. They're all standing in front of your bedroom doors." Gretchen said that her response to that was, "Well, I better wear a robe from now on!"

Gretchen described her own paranormal experience at the manor, saying, "I was in bed around two or three o'clock in the morning. The windows

The living room, where the planning of the notorious Bisbee Deportation of 1917 may have taken place. *Author's collection.*

were open and that's why I wasn't sure it wasn't the wind. But I kept hearing a bang on my bedroom door. It seemed timed, like every five minutes. My door would shake, and my dogs would go crazy. So, I googled what to do if there is a ghost! It said whatever you do, don't yell. So, I said, 'Hi, ghost. I'm not yelling at you…would you go to the hotel side? They would love to see you over there!'"

That's the only real paranormal event she has experienced, but she does get the feeling like Mr. Greenway might still be lingering. She said that he still seems to have a say about what happens around here. "I say out loud, 'Mr. Greenway if you don't want this to happen just give me a sign.'"

As we walked over to the Airbnb side during the investigation, a staff member said in passing that the day before, a vacuum started on its own. Afterward, it appeared to be broken. At that moment, I felt chills.

Throughout the ghost hunt, I recorded for EVPs. We went to room 5, where a guest woke up to a person standing over them. I did not capture

This hallway is where phantom footsteps have been heard, pacing back and forth in the wee hours of the morning. *Author's collection.*

any unusual evidence in the room, but outside in the hall, I detected a lot of supernatural energy. It was coming from the corner and in front of two other rooms at the top of the stairs. Without notice, a small pebble fell at my feet. Gretchen said that she heard it fall as well. We had no idea where that came from.

On my recording, you can hear me in the same hallway, telling the ghost, "Someone is pacing and walking around up here. Is that you? Who are you?" No answer. But as I stood in front of the doorway to room 2, the Beatles room, at the doorway looking in, I say, "Love it." Then a disembodied women's voice is heard saying, "Look inside."

While inside the same room, where a dining table is set up, I asked Gretchen if that part of the room was originally outside. She told me that it was a sleeping porch, and the main living area has one too. In my recording, an EVP of a man's voice whispers, "It was on the outside." The ghost was listening and responding to our conversation as an intelligent haunting.

A séance with Francine Powers and other mediums at Greenway Manor. *Cathy Abramson BisbeeArt Photography.*

On July 22, 2022, Gretchen held a "Dinner and a Séance" event at the Greenway Manor. Debe Branning, the Mesa MVD Ghostchaser founder and director and a paranormal author; Arizona's Hip-Historian, Marshall Shore; and I were the guest speakers and hosts. We also held two séances with about twenty-five people in attendance.

I led a pendulum communication séance and was able to connect not only with spirits of historical figures but also loved ones of those in the audience. The manor was beautifully lit by candlelight as we three sat around a small table. I asked to connect with Mr. Greenway, and he responded very quickly. He answered questions for several minutes. He communicated not only through my pendulum but also through two other mediums who were also there.

A medium named Colleen Sulzer was sitting at one of the dinner tables and began to speak and answer questions for Mr. Greenway. I asked if he was happy that Gretchen bought his home, and the pendulum began to gently swing to yes. The same woman said, "Pretty. She's pretty." I asked the spirit if he thought Gretchen was pretty. The pendulum began to swing to a very hard yes.

The spirit of Isabella Greenway was seen by medium Colleen Sulzer here in front of the piano, during the Greenway Manor séance. *Author's collection.*

I asked Greenway about his charges of the kidnapping of the strikers of the deportation; at the same time, Sulzer said, "Lies!" I immediately asked the sprit if it was a lie. The response was yes. Next, I asked if he was involved with the planning of the event. He responded yes, that they did do some of the planning in the manor's living room.

There is a top hat and cane that have been in the mansion for many years. They appear to be more than one hundred years old. They supposedly belonged to either Greenway or Roosevelt. I asked the spirit that I was still communicating with if it was his. Greenway said no. He also said it wasn't Roosevelt's and didn't know the owner. In attendance were two family members of the Allen family of the Allen Block located on Subway Street in Old Bisbee. They later told Shore that they believed the hat and cane belonged to their Uncle Charlie, as they've seen him with them in a picture. The Allen family at one time owned the mansion.

I asked Mr. Greenway if he was happy with being disinterred from his grave in Ajo to be moved to Kentucky. He moved the pendulum to a small circle, communicating that he didn't understand my question. I asked if he knew about it. The medium said "Why?" as he was still communicating through her. I explained the situation and asked if he was upset. He said no, that it was okay.

Next, I tried to communicate with Teddy Roosevelt. I got nothing. Then suddenly, Sulzer said that Isabella, Greenway's wife, was there. She was standing in the living room near the piano, watching us. She only said that she would come every now and again to see. She also communicated that Mr. Greenway did the same, to oversee things.

After communicating with the historical Bisbee figures, some family members of people in attendance came through. A father who had just passed away recently also spoke through Sulzer and my pendulum. He knew that his family members were attending the event and was waiting in line to speak to them. Another spirit came in hard and strong. Benjamin, the boyfriend of a friend named Suzanne Walsh, had tragically died in recent years, swinging that pendulum like no tomorrow. I asked Suzanne for permission to share her experience at the séance. Benjamin wanted to let her know that he was preparing their next lives together and that he was always with her.

We took a break directly after this connection and then returned to attempt another style of communication. Branning and Carolee Jackson, who was another medium in attendance, led several sessions of "glass work communication," a technique mastered in England. This included a glass with words such as yes and no on cut-out pieces arranged around the table. This style requires four participants, who put two fingers on the upside-down glass and turn it in a circular motion to receive supernatural energy.

During this session, Shore's own grandmother, named Lucille, came through and gave an extraordinary showing. According to Shore, the interaction she had with the participants mirrored who she was in real life. He said that when his grandmother would enter a room, she would do it quickly, rushing to do whatever she needed to do and then leaving. Lucille's spirit pushed the glass to her answers with a great deal of force. She answered Shore's questions and then suddenly left, making the people in the large room gasp. It was a sight to see how a loved one in spirit could come back into the living world to express her love and devotion to her grandson. It was remarkable to watch.

With the evidence I recovered from the investigation and séance at the Greenway Manor and with the acknowledgement from renowned medium Allison DuBois, we can say with certainty that it is a haunted mansion!

GREENWAY ELEMENTARY SCHOOL

There is a large campus with four individual buildings that have housed school-age students in the Warren District of Bisbee for more than one hundred years. This place is Greenway Elementary, and when its main structure was being described in the planning stages, it was said to be drawn in the most modern lines of its time. John C. Greenway, who was still the general manager of the same mining company, agreed and signed off on a deed for a large piece of property right down the street from his company mansion in the late part of 1915. Since student enrollment was overloaded, the many other schools in surrounding areas of Bisbee and the Warren District were in dire straits.

An article in the *Bisbee Daily Review* published in 1915 reported that the first individual school building would be made from concrete masonry thicker than one foot. The one-story building was to be gray, and the approximate cost of the singular structure was $14,850. The school would have maple floors and natural slate blackboards. It would have five classrooms, capable of accommodating thirty pupils, with adequate coat rooms and teacher's closets. The hallway was to be twelve feet wide, and the building would have four entrances. Plans for a principal's office, book room, kitchenette and nurse's room, plus a janitor's closet, would be included in the modern structure. Classrooms would have ceilings twelve feet high, and the windows would be eight feet tall. True to this design, the school has these parameters in the present day. The property the school was eventually built on is very spacious and furnishes large playground space and room for baseball and/or softball. Children living in the Warren, Bakerville and Mason's Addition would attend the school, which included grades up to eighth.

The children of the time were given the privilege of naming the school, as it was called the "New Warren School" for several months before the students decided on calling it Greenway. The other names included Horace Mann School and Longfellow.

According to the *Greenway Elementary Handbook*, construction began on March 31, 1916. A notice in the Bisbee newspaper in August 1916 mentioned that 150 new desks were being installed in the new schoolhouse. The first building was finished by October 1917. By the 1930s, the building, along with three more, had been painted green. The auditorium was constructed in 1952, and in 1990, a modular library was added. The cafeteria was added in 1995.

Greenway Elementary School in the Warren area of Bisbee, open since 1917. *Author's collection.*

Many children have passed through the halls and sat behind desks at this school, but there appears to be another presence that has made permanent residency within the same walls. Patric Bradshaw is a Bisbee native and a teacher's aide at Greenway. He attended the school during the early 2000s and into the middle part of that decade. Bradshaw had a lot to say about the paranormal activity he has experienced there, and during an interview, he shared his own and those of others that were passed on to him by coworkers.

Bradshaw said that in the large courtyard and in the middle of the four buildings of the school, there have been many reports of individuals seeing shadowy figures running around out of the corner of their eyes. "Things like that and an eerie feeling of being watched in the area in front of the kindergarten classrooms and in front of the kindergarten playground," stated Bradshaw. He added that most reports of seeing the shadow people have been in the evening or nighttime.

In the main building, Bradshaw said that the classroom nearest the office seems to be the most active area and gives people an uneasy feeling. One late night, a teacher was working on lesson plans and brought her dog because the school has the reputation for being creepy at night. This is when an exceptional supernatural event took place. He said the dog suddenly got up from where he was resting and walked about halfway across the room. The canine froze, and then his fur bristled up and he commenced a low and intense growl while staring at the class closet, which is more of a very narrow room with two entrances. "The dog flipped out for no apparent reason and stared at one of the closet's doorways and didn't move or stop barking. The teacher then swooped up her dog and bolted out of there. This happened in room 21," stated Bradshaw.

Bradshaw also said that a different teacher saw a full-bodied apparition in the same classroom. He explained that this instructor had the room before, and she had stated that she continuously felt negative vibes there. She also reported that on occasion, as she worked at her desk, she would look up and see an entity staring at her. When she blinked, it would dissipate. She said she never felt comfortable in that classroom.

In the wing that is closest to the cafeteria, a current teacher was working late one night and had her daughter with her. They came out of the classroom and noticed that the light was on in the men's room. "Neither of them had turned the light on, and it was pretty late and no one else should have been there…they didn't see any cars in the parking lot," said Bradshaw. He added, "The light went on by itself. After that, they said they started to

The breezeway and courtyard area of the school have heard reports of shadowy figures and ominous energy. *Patric Bradshaw.*

get an ominous feeling and left." Other people have stated that they have felt cold spots in the same bathroom.

In the same wing, Bradshaw said that he had forgotten his backpack the day before he was going on vacation. He said, "I went there early in the morning on our way out of town. As I was walking back from getting my backpack, an old intercom speaker came on and made a loud screeching sound that lasted about two seconds then shut off. That was creepy. Not sure if it was disconnected at the time, but it definitely shouldn't have made that noise at that time. It made me jump!" He said the speaker was removed recently.

My husband, Randy, has a bachelor's degree in electrical engineering and gave his theory of what may have happened at that moment. He said that a ghost may have been passing by the speaker or near it and sent off an electromagnetic field (EMF) current that flowed through the wires and made contact, causing or producing the sound. He went even further to say that your nervous system creates electrical impulses that can cause an EMF. Coincidently, this field is also believed to be created by the presence of a ghost. A word to the wise: make sure that the EMF you are picking up is not a signal from a nearby electronic device while doing a paranormal investigation.

In closing, Bradshaw said that phantom footsteps and voices are heard throughout the Greenway buildings; shadows are seen passing by the doorways and windows of the classrooms when no one else was in sight.

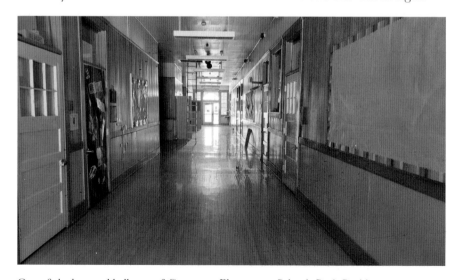

One of the haunted hallways of Greenway Elementary School. *Patric Bradshaw.*

I have no knowledge of anyone dying at the antiquated school, but someone could have loved their job so much that they could be returning. A former teacher, administrator, custodian or even an office employee could be haunting the halls and classrooms of the beloved elementary school located in a small town where people have continuously dedicated their time to the education and well-being of its children, in life and apparently in death.

EVERGREEN CEMETERY AND THE VENGEFUL GHOST KEEPING GUARD

Evergreen Cemetery has a special place in the hearts of Bisbee families whose loved ones have been laid to rest there; the hallowed grounds are sacred and cherished. This forty-plus-acre cemetery is where the bodies from the old cemetery in Brewery Gulch were transferred. It was officially established on May 3, 1912, with Ordinance 175 of the Bisbee Common Council. It is in Lowell.

There are many gorgeous tombstones—more like monuments—at the grave sites of Bisbee pioneers. There are also mausoleums for the influential families who have settled the community. Of the cemetery space, 60 percent is allocated to the several fraternal and private organizations that used to thrive in Bisbee. There is a special section for war veterans and a large religious area. There is also a large number of unmarked graves at this cemetery, evidence of the individuals who may have traveled to Bisbee from distant countries, with no kin to gift them with a deserved marker—or perhaps the persons were alone, in life and in death.

In the older section of Evergreen Cemetery, there is a family plot that is haunted by a ghost of a man who, seeking vengeance for the death of his young daughter, shot and killed a man who he thought was to blame. William C. Greene shot James C. Burnett on Allen Street in Tombstone and was later acquitted of any murder charges.

The Greene family were a substantial part of Cochise County history. Ella Roberts Greene's past has been chronicled in two different ways. Some write that she was a widow of William M. Moson from California; others say that she divorced the father of her son and daughter in 1880.

At that time, she joined her brother Ed Roberts and his family and moved to Oregon. Shortly after, they all moved to Arizona, along with a herd of horses. Ella settled along the San Pedro River and created the OR Ranch, which also housed her large herd of steer. Shortly afterward, she met her future husband, a miner named Colonel William Cornell Greene, although he was never in the military. They married in Tombstone in 1884.

The Greenes were irrigating more than one hundred acres of bottomland and had dammed the San Pedro River. One sad summer day, tragedy struck. The couple's ten-year-old daughter, also named Ella, and her friend Katie Cochran were swimming in the San Pedro River below the family dam on June 25, 1897. Swimming there was something they did often. On this day, the two girls jumped into the water without hesitation. Soon a crushing wave of water pushed them down under, and both drowned. Unbeknownst to them, Burnett had blasted the Greene dam with dynamite that day.

For several years before the tragedy, the two men had many arguments over water lawsuits. There were reports, three years before the incident, that Burnett threatened to kill Colonel Greene the first chance he got. After the death of his daughter, Greene offered $1,000 for the information of who blew up his dam.

At 1:00 p.m. on July 1, 1897, on Allen Street and near the O.K. Corral stables, Greene's gun fired three rounds, killing Burnett. Witnesses reported that Burnett's body was found facedown in a pool of blood. When his body was turned over, blood spurt from the gunshot wound in his chest.

Colonel Greene was arrested at the site and taken to jail. A reporter from the *Prospector* went to the sheriff's office just a few minutes after the shooting and took a statement from the killer. This is an excerpt of Greene's statement from the newspaper article in the *Graham Guardian*, dated July 9, 1897:

> *I have no statement to make other than that man was the cause of my child being drowned. I ascertained beyond the shadow of a doubt that he was the guilty man, and when I thought of my little girl as she put her arms around my neck on the day she drowned, I could think of nothing but vengeance on the man who caused her death. I have lived in this territory twenty-five years and have always been a peaceable, law-abiding man, I held no animosity and have no regret for anything except the death of my little girl, and the little Cochran girl and the grief of my poor wife.*

He added, "Vengeance is mine, I will repay, saith the Lord."

Greene had public sympathy in his favor. Friends and bondsmen rushed to pay for his $30,000 bond. His trial was short, as several witnesses came forward to testify against Burnett, setting Greene free from murder charges.

There was an agreement of some kind between Greene and the City of Bisbee at the time of his wife's death in December 1899. Green agreed to fence Evergreen Cemetery if the city would promise to upkeep his family plot for as long as the cemetery existed.

No such explicit agreement was ever found, but according to a 2003 article in the *Bisbee Observer*, documents were discovered that seem to match the perpetual care promise. There were reports to the city council from 1917 through 1933 of the Greene plot's condition. These included one dated from July 1917 noting that the fence around Mrs. W.C. Greene's plot was painted and grass cut twice. Another report, from June 1919, stated that the grave of Mrs. W.C. Greene had been cleaned up. In November 1923, the Greene plot was cleaned; in September 1932, it was reported that the Greene plot was looking very lovely. In September 1932, it was said that the Greene plot was looking very nice for Memorial Day. During 1965, a first-class job had been done on the Greene Cemetery plot. There were no more entries of record regarding the upkeep of the family plot after that year.

As mentioned before, Evergreen Cemetery is a much-loved site and is often visited by Bisbee residents at different times of the day. There have been reports of a white fog surrounding the Greene plot on sunshine-filled

Greene family plot in Evergreen Cemetery, where the ghost of Colonel Greene's haunts the perimeter. *Author's collection.*

days. There have also been reports of people hearing the hard footsteps of a person marching on the pavement near the plot.

Lowell School stands across the cemetery. Over the decades, there have been several accounts of lights being seen there at night. Students arriving from long-distance away games have seen eerie lights floating over graves in the cemetery in the vicinity of the Greene plot.

Individuals visiting the cemetery have witnessed, usually at a distance from the family plot, an apparition of a man walking around it. When the grave site is approached, the man disappears. Colonel Greene's ghost may be haunting the cemetery plot during the times the city isn't maintaining it and is nowhere to be seen when it is.

The family plot where the hauntings take place has a tall monument marking the grave for the young Ella. Next to her is her mother's large headstone. Colonel Greene died in 1911 and is buried in Cananea, Mexico.

THE BISBEE MASSACRE

Bisbee's Main Street in 1883 was a long and very narrow dirt road with maybe just enough room for two wagons to pass each other—about eighteen feet wide. Buildings on the street were mostly made of wood and were tightly fitted on either side of the street. Letson Block is the name of the site where two buildings are recorded as the oldest buildings on Main Street, as well as the site of the Bisbee Massacre.

In 1888, James Letson built the Mansion House Hotel, an adobe building on the left. On the right, he built the Turf Saloon in 1894. Before the Letson Block was built, the Goldwater-Castañeda Store stood at the same location.

The Bon Ton Saloon was next to the Letson Hotel in front of what is now 28 Main Street. The Goldwater-Castañeda Store is where 22 and 24 Main Street are today. Across the street is where the Hardy's Store used to stand (23 Main Street). The owner left town suddenly, leaving the store vacant for a man named John Heath (sometimes spelled "Heith"). He opened a dance hall there, according to James F. Duncan of Tombstone, a witness. Some historians say that his dance hall was not there but at 38 Main. At today's 29 Main, Annie Roberts owned a restaurant that was adjoined to two saloons. Bill Daniels owned one, and William Roberts owned the other.

On the snowy night of December 8, 1883, four people, plus an unborn child, were murdered on Main Street in Bisbee. They were shot and killed by

The site of the Bisbee Massacre of 1883. *Author's collection.*

Another view of Bisbee's Main Street, where five men killed four people and an unborn child during a robbery gone wrong. *Author's collection.*

a gang of bandits robbing the only safe in town for what they thought would be $7,000 in payroll money.

During the first week of December, five strangers were seen loitering around town, keeping a low profile. At seven o'clock on the evening of December 8, these same five men rode up Mule Gulch with old bandanas covering their faces. They passed the smelter and dismounted their horses at Preston's Lumberyard, near to where the library and post office are today. From there, they made their way to the Goldwater Castañeda Store on the same side of the street.

Two of the men, Dan Dowd and Billy Delaney, stationed themselves on the sidewalk at the entrance to the store. There was a delivery wagon parked in front. Dan Kelly, Red Sample and Tex Howard entered the store. As soon as those men entered, they yelled for everyone inside to raise their hands in the air.

José Miguel Castañeda, who was the store manager, was at the back of the store near a bedroom door. Thinking fast, he grabbed several hundred dollars and went into the back room. He placed the money under the pillow, lay down on the bed and faked being sick. Tex Howard followed him and screamed and pushed at him to get up. Then he took his cash and shoved Castañeda back into the store.

In the meantime, Red Sample had Joe Goldwater open the safe. Sample told Goldwater, "Get the payroll."

Goldwater answered, "That's where you're fooled. The stagecoach is late. The money is not here."

Sample pushed Goldwater aside and helped himself to some Mexican money and some valuables belonging to several Bisbee residents.

Outside, two Bisbee men, John Tappiner and Joseph Bright, came out of the Bon Ton Saloon and started to go past Dowd and Delaney as they walked up the street. Delaney commanded the two men to go into the store. Tappiner said that he would not and turned to go back in the saloon. Bright started to run up the street, with Dowd firing after him.

Delaney's first shot missed Tappiner, but the second shot hit him in the head, tearing away a portion of his skull and leaving his brains running off the porch of the Bon Ton Saloon, where he fell.

While this was happening, a volunteer fireman named James Krigbaum and some others ran out of the alley in between the bank building and 5 Main and started shooting at the bandits. Krigbaum took aim at one of the tall outlaws and fired, grazing his coat.

Next to the Goldwater-Castañeda Store was Joe Mary's Saloon, where a man named Howard stepped out and was gunned down instantly. This spot is now in front of 18 and 20 Main Street.

At this time, a deputy from New Mexico named Tom Smith was with his wife eating supper in Sima's restaurant, (25 Main Street). Deputy Smith came out, ordered them to quit shooting and told them that he was a lawman. Delaney told him, "You're the man we're lookin for." He then shot Smith in the left shoulder.

Deputy Smith remarked, "I am hit."

Delaney said, "I will give you another."

The second shot killed Smith. The deputy's body was found between the shafts of the delivery wagon. After being shot the second time, he crawled through from the back of the wagon and died.

The story of the next victim is a shocking and sad one. An eight-month-pregnant Annie Roberts was standing at the door of her restaurant (29 Main Street) when the shooting began. She came to peek at what was causing the commotion outside. When she turned to go back in the building, one of the balls from Dowd's gun missed Bright and passed through the doorjamb, lodging in the small of her back. Roberts died in terrible agony the next morning.

J.A. Nolly was in a saloon (21 Main) when the shooting started. He ran out and was shot by Dowd in the belly. Nolly died the following week.

After that, the gang managed to get out of town, while two Bisbee men, Bill Daniels and John Reynolds, ran down the gulch with guns blazing, chasing the bandits. They didn't manage to hit a single target. The Bisbee Massacre lasted a total of about fifteen minutes.

Immediately, Krigbaum was sent to Tombstone. The *Bisbee Review* said that he made it there on his horse in about two hours. Ironically, on the way he passed the stagecoach with the $7,000 the gang was after.

A posse was organized the same night with forty-five to fifty men. Daniels and John Heath were part of the search party. When the posse reached a fork in the road at Forest Ranch, Heath tried to convince the others that the gang must be heading north toward the Dragoons or even Tombstone. The others disagreed strongly and headed toward Sulphur Springs Valley and the Chiricahua Mountains instead. Heath went north.

The posse was on the gang's trail, which led them to the ranch of Dan Ross. Near the Ross house, there was a large crevice in the rock, twenty to twenty-five feet deep. Here the posse found the carcasses of horses. They had been run almost to death. The bandits stripped them of their bridles and saddles and brutally shoved them into the crevice, leaving them there to die. They then walked, carrying their saddles and bridles, into the ranch of Frank Buckles, where they camped for several days before they stole his horses.

After that appalling discovery, the posse continued trekking and stopped at the cabin of Luben Pardu. Pardu said that five men stopped at his place, divided up some money and items and then left in different directions. He also said that another man and the same group had been at his cabin a week before. The other man seemed to act like the leader of the group. He named all five men, plus John Heath as their leader. Heath was quickly found in Bisbee and taken to Tombstone.

Eventually, months later, the men were caught. On February 8, 1884, the defendants were brought into court to make their pleas. Each pleaded not guilty. Heath was tried alone. On February 17, 1884, at 8:00 p.m., the jurors gave Heath the verdict of guilty of murder in the second degree. On February 21, he was sentenced to life imprisonment. I cover the results of what happened to the bandits and to Heath after their capture in the Tombstone chapter of this book. To say the least, it is incredibly interesting and horrifying.

Bisbee's Main Street is different compared to how it was back in 1883. All the buildings were made of wood but now are made of brick, adobe or cement. Of course, the street is paved, and because of the buildings and their proximity, sound bounces very well, with lots of echo.

In the evening hours, especially when the road seems silent, a plague of sadness can overwhelm you as you stroll past each of the sites where innocent people were gunned down. In front of the old E.W. Woolworth Company's variety store building, there have been reports of a woman's low bellowing cry during the earliest morning hours. Along with that sound comes a young man's voice, calling out inaudible words to her. It seems that the female voice ignores his and continues to weep, causing echoes of misery along the narrow street.

With such a degree of pain and suffering, it is not surprising to hear phantasmal cries and see dark shadows forming and disappearing on Main Street. The eerie noises are best heard in the wee hours of the night.

Bisbee's Main Street will likely be one of the most fascinating and gorgeous roads in Arizona for years to come, regardless of the historical event that took place there.

TOMBSTONE

If you were to stroll down the wooden sidewalks on Allen Street in Tombstone, Arizona, you might feel as if you were floating back in time, back to the American Wild West days during the late 1800s, when unutterable deaths transpired—some would call it the actual beginning of the town's now legendary hauntings.

Tombstone's town founder is a man named Ed Schieffelin, who discovered silver and founded a community that has the title of the "Town Too Tough to Die." Schieffelin was on an exploration of the Arizona Territory that included the hills of what was called Goose Flats. He traveled with a group that included Hualapai scouts, who were under the command of the U.S. Army and moving to what is now Fort Huachuca. The group was seeking rebel Chiricahua Apaches in the area.

Eventually, Schieffelin decided to head out on his own to get more serious time to prospect, but the soldiers he had spent much time with would tease him and warn him that the only thing he would find in the southern part of the territory was his tombstone.

Schieffelin, his brother Al and a man named Richard Gird set out to find the treasure of precious ore in the region. They found what they were looking for, and soon their mining operation grew, as the ore samples they found assayed out to $2,000 per ton. Tombstone grew into a densely populated city almost immediately. By 1879, the most successful silver mines were making dividends of $50,000 per month, which lasted for about two years.

Tombstone's Allen Street, one of the most visited places in the American Wild West. *Author's collection.*

Pumping water out of the mines was a problem in 1881—2.5 million gallons of water were pumped out per day. As the national economy fluctuated, along with the price of silver, so did the opulence in Tombstone. After the pumps failed and the price of silver dropped in 1889, local mining operations ceased. The mines were reopened in 1902 and stayed open until 1923, when they were permanently closed.

Tombstone regained its popularity through books, movies and television shows depicting its attractive and rowdy past during the 1950s and throughout the 1960s. Some recent movies, such as 1992's *Tombstone* and 1994's *Wyatt Earp*, made the town a popular place to visit for one's "bucket list."

THE SITE OF JOHN HEATH'S LYNCHING

On February 21, 1884, John Heath was led into court and was given a sentence to serve life at the territorial prison in Yuma for his participation in the Bisbee Massacre. Several Bisbee citizens were worried that he would live long enough to be pardoned. They decided to take the law into their own hands to avoid the possibility that Heath would take his case to the U.S. Supreme Court.

A Committee of Safety, called "45/60," announced that "John Heath was guilty as hell and deserved the same punishment as the others."

On the morning of February 22, 1884, the committee, made up of some of the most influential Bisbee citizens and miners, traveled to Tombstone and, at 8:00 a.m., marched to the jail unmasked. They were met with more men from the Contention and the Grand Central mines.

At that point, a select number of seven men from Bisbee went to the door leading to the jail and knocked, yelling to let them in. Two men kicked at the jail's gate, and chief jailer Billy Ward opened the door on their demand. The jailer was expecting breakfast for the prisoners at that time and answered unarmed. Instantly the jailor was staring right into numerous gun barrels and was ordered to hand over the keys. Ward didn't resist and handed them over. The men opened Heath's cell, unshackled him and led him out into a hall of the jail.

They grabbed Heath, and a rope held by several men was placed around his waist. It was reported that the group's first intention was to hang him immediately from the banister of the stairs leading to the second story of the

The location in the Tombstone Courthouse, where John Heath's cell would have been located back in 1884. *Author's collection.*

building of the jail, but the larger part of the crowd was already heading to a telegraph pole just a little farther up the road.

Right as Heath and the crowd got to the front of the door of the courthouse, they were met by Sherriff Ward, who began shouting in a strong voice of authority, "Stop this! You have got to stop this right here!"

Without hesitancy, the sheriff was picked up and thrown down the stairs by an unidentified individual as the crowd continued with its mission. They dragged Heath and ran down Toughnut Street to a point below where the railroad crosses the street. The rope was then hung on the telegraph pole.

Upon arrival, witnesses say that Heath pulled a handkerchief from his pocket and said these words: "Boys, you are hanging an innocent man, and you will find it out before those other men are hung. Tie this handkerchief over my eyes. I am not afraid to die. I have one favor to ask, that you will not mutilate my body by shooting into it after I am hung."

His request was followed, and his eyes were covered; in an instant, he was strung up and was dead. His body was left dangling from the rope hanging from the cross bar on the telegraph pole. His body hung there for many hours before it was taken down and sent to the county physician's office of Dr. George Goodfellow.

Heath's death certificate reads, "John Heath came to his death from emphysema of the lungs, a disease common in high altitudes, which might have been caused by strangulation, self-inflicted or otherwise."

On February 19, 1884, the five bandits were sentenced for the murders, and on March 25, each was hanged by the neck until dead. The graves of the five members of the gang are in the Boothill Cemetery located in Tombstone; there is also a marker for Heath.

According to the *Herald* newspaper in an announcement about Heath's hanging printed on February 28, 1884, a place card was posted on the telegraph pole where his body was found suspended and dead. The card had the following inscription:

> JOHN HEITH *was hanged to this pole by the* CITIZENS OF COCHISE COUNTY *for participation in the Bisbee massacre as a proved accessory at 8:20 A.M., February 22, 1884 (Washington's Birthday)*

At the Tombstone Courthouse, State Park Manager Curtis Leslie told me, "When they first built the jail, it had twelve cells. Eight were wood, while four were made of steel. When they extended the jail, it had sixteen cells." Outside at the prison yard, Leslie showed me where the original jail was and the extension in 1903, where there are different-looking bricks seen on the building of the prison yard. He pointed out the location of the original door in which the prisoners would exit. Now there is a prominent outline of that door on the exterior wall.

Heath hangs from a telegraph pole after a Bisbee mob put its version of "street justice" into action. *Author's collection.*

Left: State Park Manager Curtis Leslie demonstrating where the original door was during the time of Heath's lynching and where he was dragged out by a Bisbee mob. *Author's collection.*

Opposite: Today, there is a plaque and telegraph pole stump memorializing the hanging of Heath and the place his ghost may still be lingering. *Author's collection.*

At the site of the lynching, the original telegraph pole used has been removed, but a stump was left in its place. Right next to the stump is a plaque that reads, "John Heath was taken from the jail by a mob and hanged at this location on February 22, 1884."

William Woolwine, a paranormal investigator like myself, had been to the site of Heath's lynching numerous times, leaving with no solid evidence of a haunting. Woolwine, who is with Hauntings Encounters Adventures, said

A poignant image of John Heath's grave marker at Boothill Graveyard. *Author's collection.*

that he would not give up. He used a structured light sensor camera (SLS), which records and picks up on forms of energy. The camera translates or maps out the energy forms into stick figures. These can be interpreted to be actual ghosts. The camera works through an infrared light projector with a monochrome CMOS sensor that translates as dots manipulated in 3D formations. The inferred dots allow the camera to exhibit depth as the software projects the stick figures with joints and movements.

He said that he had a feeling about the site and finally captured a full-bodied apparition with the camera. As Woolwine and I spoke about his evidence, I said that it is very sad if John Heath is still lingering there after all this time. Woolwine agreed.

TOMBSTONE COURTHOUSE

On February 15, 1881, the Cochise County supervisors passed an act to authorize the purchase of land, erect and furnish a courthouse and jail and issue bonds to provide for the monies. During that same year, Tombstone's population reached ten thousand, putting the town in contention for the county seat. Tucson at the time held that title for Pima County, and the town of Prescott was the territorial capital. Tombstone's political power began to strengthen as the population grew. In 1881, the Arizona legislature created Cochise County; because of Tombstone's growth, it became the county seat. Tombstone held the county seat until 1929, when it moved to Bisbee, as it was then the most populated and gained residents and votes for the change. The Tombstone Courthouse officially closed in 1931 upon the opening of the new county courthouse in Bisbee.

The courthouse was built in 1882 and cost about $50,000. The two-story building is in the shape of a Roman cross and sits on the corner of Toughnut and Second Streets. The building housed the board of supervisors office as well as those of the county treasurer and recorder, the sheriff's department and the district attorney. Adjoining the treasurer's and recorder's office are fireproof vaults. It also had a jailor's room and a jail made for twelve prison cells at the rear of the building positioned under the courtroom.

Besides the interior of the courthouse, there also was a courtyard for the prisoners held in the jail, and on demand, a wooden scaffold or gallows could be constructed at an end of the lawn. Legal hangings took place on the

The Tombstone Courthouse State Historic Park and Cochise County's first courthouse. *Author's collection.*

The replica of the gallows of Cochise County, sitting on the actual site of the historical executions of seven men. *Randy G. Powers.*

gallows and were made part of public record, including the explicit details of how each man died and how long it took for him to die. Seven men were executed there, as capital punishment was a role of county government until in 1912, when Arizona became a state.

The building was listed in the National Register of Historic Places in 1972 and is the Tombstone Courthouse State Historic Park. It was second to be designated as a state park in 1959 but was the first to open following the establishment of the Arizona State Parks Board of 1957. Tubac was the first park, but at the time it wasn't ready to be opened.

Curtis Leslie is park manager of the courthouse. He told me that after the building closed as a courthouse, they tried different things with it. He said, "They tried to make it into a hotel but that didn't happen, and it was eventually abandoned by the '40s. By the '50s, the Tombstone Restoration Committee helped save this building because it was in disrepair. They even tried to make it into a three-level building at the time it was being attempted to be used as a hotel." He added that the building stood vacant until 1955 and then became a state park in 1959.

When the restoration commission acquired the old courthouse, it restored the building and created the historical museum that has continuously operated since 1959. It now displays thousands of artifacts and exhibits telling the story of Tombstone and Cochise County's early history.

I inquired about where John Heath and the other Bisbee Massacre bandits would've been kept. Leslie said that his cell would've been in front of the Mining Room at the south side of the building.

Even though the park has plans showing where the cells were according to the park manager, the exact location is still a little foggy. At the entryway of the Mining Room, in 1903, they extended the building back a few feet into what the entry of that mining-themed room is now. Leslie explained that the hall in which we were standing was where the actual cells would have been located.

A close replica of the gallows now stands as a reminder of the Wild West days of Cochise County. Leslie said, "They were torn down in 1912 because that is when Arizona became a state. The county no longer did executions. The original gallows were burned in 1912 at the time the state took over the execution of malefactors from the counties." He added, "The gallows at the courthouse were only put up when there was going to be an execution. They had to put them up a couple of times. There was a couple more times the gallows were set up but there was a stay of execution, or a prisoner escaped. The structure would not be up when prisoners were out."

On March 28, 1884, due to the Bisbee Massacre, Dan Dowd, Dan Kelly, Red Sample, James Howard and William Delaney were hanged simultaneously. The night before their execution, they had a luscious dinner including oysters and other delicacies provided by Sheriff Ward. After their meal, they had a restless night and didn't get much sleep in anticipation to the morning's planned event. A man named Will Baron was admitted into their jail cell early in the morning to give them a close shave, and then they were dressed in clean black suits, again furnished by the sheriff.

Nellie Cashman and a few reverends were in attendance when Sheriff Ward read the death warrant in their jail cell. The men listened attentively as the sheriff read in a clear, firm voice. After the reading of the warrant, he said that he would allow their request to be free of any type of restraints on their way to the scaffolds and to their marks.

More than five hundred tickets to see the hangings were issued by Sheriff Ward, and the courthouse yard was packed. The gate to the jail yard was opened at noon, and at 1:10 p.m., the procession of the gang from the jail to the gallows began. Each condemned man was escorted by either a religious man or Cochise County deputy. The procession moved from the jail door to the foot of the gallows, leading up nine steps to the platform, ascended in silence. Five chairs were placed then they were seated.

The prisoners looked nervously around the crowd and then at the dangling nooses. Delaney, Kelly and Sample recognized familiar faces in the crowd and shouted in a sarcastic, cheerful voice, "Goodbye!" Moments later, their arms and legs were strapped. Then Sheriff Ward said, "Stand up, boys." They stood up in sync, and the chairs were removed. This is when Sample said, "I die innocent of the murders and robbery committed at Bisbee and as far as I know, John Heath had nothing to do with the affair. I die in a firm belief in the Catholic church and request a Christian burial." The other four men protested in the same manner.

Ward asked if they had anything else to say, and they all answered no. The nooses were then adjusted around their necks by officials as priests whispered words of consolation into their ears. Dowd remarked that the noose was a regular choking machine. Black hoods of cloth were pulled down over their faces and the nooses tightened. Kelly said with a muffled voice, "Let her go."

At exactly 1:18 p.m., Sheriff Ward cut the rope that was holding a 255-pound weight that was suspended and holding the platform trapdoor. It fell with a swishing sound and an echoing bang as it struck the framework of the scaffold. The five men shot downward, and when the ropes became tight, the platform shook with the descending weight as the lumber creaked. The suspended bodies were frozen, except for Dowd, whose body convulsed as he suffocated.

The men hung there for thirty minutes. They were then pronounced dead and were cut down and placed in plain coffins. The physicians concluded that apart from Sample, the necks of the executed men hand not been dislocated.

On November 16, 1900, William and Thomas Halderman were executed in the courtyard. The Haldermans were brothers who, in a most dramatic way, resisted arrest and shot and killed Deputy Ainsworth and Constable Moore on April 6, 1899, in the Chiricahua Mountains. They were convicted of murder in the first degree and were originally sentenced to be hanged at the Tombstone gallows on August 10 of the same year.

The murders of Cochise County deputy Chester L. Ainsworth and Constable Edward "Ted" Moore were described in the *Arizona Republican* in an article titled "COLD-BLOODED MURDER." They were shot and killed by William Halderman, twenty-six, and Thomas Halderman, twenty-three. William was a Cochise County resident for two years, coming from Hanover, New Mexico. Thomas claimed to be a resident of Davis, DeWitt County, in Texas.

Ironically, the Haldermans were known to be friendly with Deputy Ainsworth. The two brothers lived on a cattle ranch about thirty-five miles from Pearce, near a small community named Wilgus. Deputy Ainsworth had a warrant for them for killing cattle on the range. The deputy set out to the Halderman ranch that April morning then stopped at the Moore residence to enlist the aid of the nineteen-year-old.

The two were armed with pistols, even though they didn't anticipate any type of trouble from the brothers. When the officers arrived, the Haldermans were in the yard. Deputy Ainsworth made the formal arrest without any resistance. The deputy asked the two men if they had eaten breakfast yet. The brothers said they hadn't. The deputy told them to go ahead inside the house and eat. They followed his order. They were also advised that they would most likely be staying in Pearce for two to three days for their preliminary examination and that they should make ample preparations.

The two officers rested easily on their horses near the house as they waited. After some time, Deputy Ainsworth called to one of the brothers by his first name and asked if they were ready. No reply was made, but without warning, the two brothers bolted out from different doors. One ended up in front of Ainsworth, while the other made his way behind him. Armed with Winchesters, the Halderman brothers opened fire simultaneously on the deputy.

A bullet grazed the front of Ainsworth's left shoulder, while another entered the back of his head and came out just beneath the right eye. The deputy fell from his horse, and then the two brothers turned their rifles on Moore.

Moore was shot in his stomach but did not die on the spot. He drew his pistol and shot four bullets, missing both men. Constable Moore saw that his partner was dead and was able to jump on his horse and make it to his home, where he met his mother and sister. He told them about the shooting, but unfortunately, he died about two hours afterward.

The brothers took Ainsworth's horse and one of their own and escaped into the mountains. The deputy's body was found in the snow during the time Moore's family contacted authorities. Ainsworth's body was accompanied by his brother, Arizona attorney general Chauncey Ainsworth, to Flint, Michigan. Moore was buried near his home.

A posse consisting of fifty men searched the mountains for the brothers, but they were found in New Mexico and brought to Tombstone on April 24,

1899. When interviewed by a reporter, they talked freely, and both admitted to the murders, although they believed that they were justified in killing the officers. William Halderman admitted to being on unfriendly terms with Moore but refused to say more about the trouble he had with him. They told the reporter that they walked from the scene of the murders in the Chiricahuas to the Hill Ranch, which was thirty miles from Lordsburg, because they couldn't catch the horses.

Upon hearing their sentence to be hanged, the brothers had no response. While leaving the courtroom, William Halderman saw an old friend seated near the aisle, and as he passed him, he loudly said, "A good shot, eh?" Then when the officers and the brothers reached the stairway, the same brother stubbed his foot against the carpet, bringing the procession to a stop. William said, "We are wearing our shoes out traveling up and down these stairs Tom." Thomas thought it was funny and laughed and smiled. After they went back to their cells, they began a game of cards.

The brothers were first tried and convicted on June 20, 1899, to be hanged on August 25 of the same year. An appeal was allowed by the U.S. Supreme Court, which sustained the finding of the lower court. Secretary Akers, who was the acting governor, refused to grant another respite. They were again sentenced, and another day was set for the execution on August 10, 1900. Surprisingly, days before the execution was to take place, President William McKinley interfered and granted a further respite until October 5. Then Governor Murphy extended the respite until noon of November 16, 1900. The men were executed at 12:38 p.m. that day.

The Halderman brothers were hanged in front of about 150 people at the gallows in the Tombstone Courthouse yard. The brothers were said to be courageous as they climbed the scaffold, showing no signs of fear. While on the scaffold, William jokingly said as he looked down, "This is a nice-looking crowd." At that moment, Thomas placed the rope around his own neck and said that he was ready. Both professed to be Christian and asked the crowd to pray for them.

Sheriff Scott read the death warrant and then asked if they wished to make a statement. Thomas said, "I have nothing to say, and it wouldn't do any good anyhow."

William said, "This will be an experience that ought to benefit you all." The cap was then pulled over their heads, and both said goodbye. Fifteen minutes later, they were pronounced dead.

Paranormal activity at the Tombstone Courthouse seems inevitable because, like the Bisbee Courthouse, a lot of emotional traumas has

Left: An EVP was recorded of a demonic voice right next to these gallows. *Author's collection.*

Below: The Tombstone courtroom has heard reports of phantom voices and the sound of the pounding of a judge's gavel. *Author's collection.*

unfolded there. Except here there were executions as well. I spent a few hours at the courthouse recently and found it very intriguing; I eagerly consumed the history involving the building and the history of southern Arizona. I was lucky enough to get some time alone in the courtyard and did some ghost hunting.

I recorded videos, took pictures and then used my hand-held recorder for an EVP session. A few days later, I found on one of my videos, at the beginning, a deep, whispering growl from a disembodied voice saying, "Hello." This made me fall back from my office chair. I believe this was not a ghost, but a demonic presence.

Other paranormal activity has been reported at the Tombstone Courthouse. When Leslie was asked about any supernatural experiences he has had or those that guests have shared with him, he said that the most common site for paranormal experiences is in the courtroom. He said that he gets people who occasionally have a weird feeling in that area of the building.

Jeff Woolwine, of Haunted Encounters Adventures, was in the courtroom of the courthouse doing a ghost hunt and had a similar communication with what seemed to be an intelligent haunting. Woolwine and his wife, Pam, had done an EVP session in the courtroom with a sprit box and were able to strike a conversation with a few entities. Woolwine told me that as he was setting up the spirit box, he was recording himself on video. He didn't realize it until he got back home to analyze his evidence, finding that his camera mic had captured what sounded like a room full of people. There was no one else there. His camera also caught audio of banging, similar to the sound of a judge's gavel.

"I was tripping out when I heard the sounds of people and the banging, since nobody was in the courtroom with me," said Woolwine.

Woolwine does paranormal videos on YouTube under the name Haunted Encounters Adventures, and during the recording, you can hear disembodied voices coming through the spirit box in the courtroom. Almost immediately, voices started to vibrate from the contraption as he tuned it. The voices repeated "hello" a few times, and then Woolwine asked their name. At first, the voice asked, "What?" Then the first voice said, "Joseph." There was a pause of silence until the ghost said for Woolwine to speak. Then he asked, "Who is here?"

The ghost said, "Me" and "I am."

Woolwine asked, "What is your name?" The answer was, "Dowd." As soon as I heard that name, I made the connection to one of the men hanged with his involvement in the Bisbee Massacre!

The Tombstone Courthouse, once filled with the light of justice, now sits quietly, seemingly haunted by fervent energies from a time gone by. *Randy G. Powers.*

At this point, the voices were speaking backward. Woolwine said that in situations like this, he would reverse the video or audio to a MP3, which makes the recording sound normal. Through this process, he could make out what the ghost was saying.

The voice now sounded like a man's voice and answered the question of who was there in the building. "We're outside."

Woolwine asked if there was anyone who wanted to talk. The ghost answered, "Don't let me out."

He asked the ghost if there is anyone else who wants to talk with us. The ghost replied, "Will's outside."

There may be a fantastic connection to the same EVP I caught at the gallows. This deep growling voice may very well be that of William Halderman or William Delaney!

During this investigation, Woolwine used his SLS camera and picked up on figures near the spiral staircase and in different rooms of the building. Although he did seem to catch apparitions on camera elsewhere in the courthouse, he says he thinks the courtroom is indeed haunted.

The courtrooms are filled with lingering energy from traumatic events and ancient emotions from the past. Many other people who have visited have said they have heard voices when no one else is in the room with them—a recording of time, replaying itself into eternity. The courtroom seems to have intelligent as well as residual hauntings.

BIRD CAGE THEATRE

Tombstone is home to one of the most renowned theaters of the West Coast, first opened by Lottie and William Hutchingson. This place is the notorious Bird Cage Theatre, and between 1881 and 1889, the establishment was considered to be the roughest, bawdiest and most wicked night spots on the Pacific coast. This rowdy and very successful business opened its doors during December 1881 and closed in 1889.

It was opened twenty-four hours a day, and the longest poker game ever recorded was held in the basement. The minimum to get into this game was $1,000. The poker game went on, night and day, for eight years, five months and three days.

The stage is hand-painted and pays tribute to the great entertainers who performed there, such as Nellie Boyd, Robert McWade, Lola Montez and

Top: A picturesque scene on Allen Street as a stagecoach passes by the infamous Bird Cage Theatre. *Jonathon Donahue.*

Bottom: A card table at the Bird Cage Theatre memorializes the longest poker game played in history. *Author's collection.*

A bordello-style room downstairs at the Bird Cage Theatre. *Author's collection.*

the Shakespearean actor Frederick Warde. The main hall has a fifteen- by-fifteen-foot stage that is five feet above the floor.

The working women at the theater were waitresses and prostitutes. There were bordello-style rooms downstairs, and upstairs there were fourteen private "boxes" positioned over the main hall. These were also used for viewing entertainment on the stage below. There were seven on each side of the room, and they had red velvet curtains that could be drawn when private activity was being provided. There was also a dumbwaiter used to hoist up saloon goods, such as drinks and cigars to the guests in the box seats.

Arthur J. Lamb, a writer and composer during the early 1880s, said he thought the cribs that were overhanging the casino reminded him of a birdcage. He thought that the girls with the feathers in their hair, serving kisses and champagne, were like birds in a gilded cage. Lamb had Harry Von Tilzer write the musical arrangement for the song "She's Only a Bird in a Gilded Cage." The famous singer Lillian Russell sang the song, which became one of the most popular melodies of the nineteenth century.

Of course, with the kind of environment that included gambling and whatever comes with the tenderloin business, there's drama. The Bird

The infamous Bird Cage box seats, where a variety of services were offered and received. *Author's collection.*

Cage has one of the juiciest and most legendary stories, one that has captivated people's interest for more than one hundred years. The legend of Gold Dollar and Margarita's love triangle, involving a man named Billy Milgreen, is infamous.

Gold Dollar was a prostitute who earned that nickname due to her blonde hair and for the gold coin from her era. She was in a romantic relationship with Milgreen, who was a neurotic gambler and a regular at the theater. Things were going great for the couple until a young Mexican prostitute arrived at the Bird Cage. She was different-looking compared to the other woman in Tombstone, as she had long dark hair and an olive complexion. She was very attractive, and regardless of the many men who became infatuated with her, she liked Milgreen the most.

During one night at the theater, while Gold Dollar was working over at the Crystal Palace, Margarita saw the opportunity to seize the moment with Milgreen, as he was alone. She sat on his lap as he played at the card table and flirted heavily, with Milgreen happily accepting her affections. Word got to Gold Dollar, and as anyone would have expected from the hothead, she sprinted to the theater and, upon arrival, instantly spotted the two and became even more enraged.

Margarita didn't know what was coming, and before she could even let a scream out, Gold Dollar grabbed her long black hair and pulled her off Milgreen. Without thinking twice, the blond woman stabbed Margarita with a very slender dagger, killing her instantly. According to legend, Gold Dollar was never charged, and the weapon was never found. There is a grave over at Boothill marking the young woman's body.

This and so many more stories of murder, shootings, stabbings and thieving at the Bird Cage have saturated the very walls of the ancient building with dark impressions. This site is one of the most haunted places on this planet. By the time it closed, 140 bullet holes had been left in the walls and ceilings of the establishment. The Bird Cage also boasts that twenty-six people may have been killed there. This is the perfect scenario for paranormal activity.

Countless witnesses have seen ghosts and dark shadows. Phantom music from the era of the late 1880s has been heard by several witnesses. Ghosts of cowboys in full gear have been spotted and will vanish right before your eyes. The scent of cigars has been experienced, regardless of the "no smoking" rule in the building. Also, a strong smell of whiskey will be picked up when no one is around, and ghostly laughter has been heard throughout the building at different times of the day and night.

Then there is Margarita. She has been seen as a full-bodied apparition that fits her description perfectly, still looking like no other, even in death. Witnesses have reported seeing the young woman opening a curtain of one of the boxes upstairs in almost no clothing. Her silhouette is very feminine, and men find it attractive and seductive.

Various shadows are also seen walking across the stage and described as dark fogs in a human shape, gliding and floating. Employees have also claimed to have been touched by invisible entities.

In fact, a similar experience happened to Wendy Clark from the GHOST Crew (Ghost Hunters of Southern Tucson). While in the main hall and stage area of the building, her group was holding an investigation and was playing dance hall and saloon music to get a reaction from any ghosts that might be lurking. As the music was playing through a member's phone, Clark went to the stage area and started to move around and dance to the music.

The group's various ghost hunting equipment began to light up, and Clark said that she started to feel as if something was around her—whoever it was was dancing with her. She said she stopped dancing, but the music continued to play in the background as she started to ask questions out loud. Clark said she started to ask about the cowboys and began to make flirty comments hoping for a response. She said she was the only one on the floor, with another group member sitting on the steps that led up to the stage.

"I'm doing the flirty little thing, making comments, then I feel something, totally 'goose' me! I said whoa! Then I turned around to see if one of the guys had snuck up behind me. When I did turn around, there was no one behind me!" commented Clark. She said it felt so real, and she really thought that someone was right behind her. She added, "That was probably the best thing that has happened to me during an investigation. To be goosed!"

If you get a chance to visit the Bird Cage Theatre on Allen Street, you might catch a glimpse of the people who lived hard and died in place that is inundated with grief, pain, immorality and loneliness. It's a ghost hunter's dream.

O.K. CORRAL

The shootout at the O.K. Corral is one the most recorded events in American history. October 26, 1881, is the day that marks one of the most famous gunfights ever reported. The shootout at the O.K. Corral included three brothers, Virgil, Morgan and Wyatt Earp, plus Doc Holliday. The men they fought against included Frank and Tom McLaury, along with Ike and Billy Clanton. The O.K. Corral is now owned by Robert Love and has been in his family since 1963, and it was originally built in 1879. The "OK" stands for "Old Kindersley."

I spoke with Love, and he said that his father, Harold, and another investor took an interest in Tombstone, along with many other landmark sites in the town, and geared their history as attractions for tourists, making sure to keep it authentic.

"Although, until a point when my father bought the corral the city had signs up by the back-alley entrance to the O.K. Corral, incorrectly locating the gunfight. So, the actual location of the gunfight had pretty much been lost by probably the '30s," remarked Love.

The corral owner said that on Freemont and Third Street, there was a building on that corner called the Harwood House; it was later a vacant lot and then Fly's Gallery and Boarding House. In recent times, Love rebuilt Fly's Gallery and the other building exactly where they were located according to insurance maps of the time.

The O.K. Corral has a prominent place in Cochise County and in American history. *Author's collection.*

Above: Randy G. Powers, *center*, with the reenactors at the O.K. Corral several years ago. This site is still number one on the bucket lists of tourists from around the world. *Author's collection.*

Opposite: Wyatt Earp drew this map, the holy grail to the truth behind the actual events of the gunfight at the O.K. Corral. *O.K. Corral.*

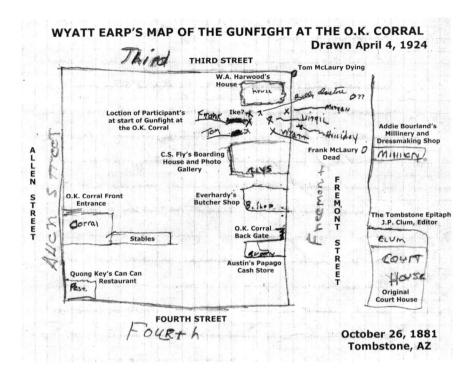

WYATT EARP'S MAP OF THE GUNFIGHT AT THE O.K. CORRAL
Drawn April 4, 1924

October 26, 1881
Tombstone, AZ

"My father went back to the newspaper reports and court records and confirmed that the gunfight actually began in the empty lot between Fly's Gallery and the Hardwood House," stated Love. He said there was a lot of misinformation after the gunfight, but he has the map drawn by Wyatt Earp. With that valuable piece of information and through the newspaper accounts of where the participants were during the event, he feels that he has the correct location.

He added, "Of course, there is a lot we don't know. Doc Holliday was rooming in Fly's Boarding House. That morning, Ike Clanton had come looking for Doc, aiming to kill him. But he wasn't there. Our assumption is that the Cowboys were waiting in the vacant lot next to Fly's because they were waiting to confront Doc Holliday. That he would be there, and Doc would be alone."

According to Love, for most years the gunfight was just called the "Earp, Clanton Gunfight." There was a movie released in the late 1950s called *Gunfight at the O.K. Corral*. This was the beginning of how the gunfight famously became correlated with the corral. Love states that when his family bought the site, they trademarked the name.

The O.K. Corral site housed various other businesses over the years; at one time, it was a car repair shop called Jack Main's Garage. *OK Corral.*

Love said, "But at the time we bought the O.K. Corral, it was broke. It was bankrupt, and the owners owed taxes to the government. There was a restaurant there instead, and after you eat, they might let you go in the back and look where the gunfight took place."

Love explained that there were two rival newspapers at the time of the event, the *Tombstone Epitaph* and the *Tombstone Nugget*. The *Epitaph* was owned by John Clum, who was the mayor of the town. Love said, "He was a Republican. He hired fellow Republican Virgil Earp to be the town's marshal. He supported the Earps. The *Nugget* supported the Cowboys."

In April 1881, the Tombstone City Council passed an ordinance declaring that all pistols, rifles and Bowie knifes were to be stored at a livery or saloon soon after coming into town. "There was gun control in Tombstone. When you arrived in town, you had to store your gun. For example, if you came to the O.K. Corral, you would leave it in the office, otherwise you could leave it at the local bar or hotel. But you were not allowed to carry guns in town," said Love.

He also stated, "But the *Nugget* tried to argue that the Cowboys were about to leave town and that's why they had guns. The *Nugget* started calling the gunfight near or at the O.K. Corral, because they wanted to make it

The *Tombstone Epitaph* heavily covered the famous shootout at the O.K. Corral, and the newspaper is still in business. The Epitaph Building may also be haunted. Burton Webster from the *Epitaph* said that the building's camera monitors have recorded shadows moving after hours. After securing the building, nobody is ever found. *From the* Tombstone Epitaph.

out that the Cowboys were leaving town. There was no proof that was the case. That's why it became associated with the O.K. Corral and the idea the Cowboys were leaving town."

According to the information I gathered from an endless number of newspaper articles and historical books regarding the gunfight and from information shared by Love, the trouble began when two men with the last names of Stilwell and Spencer were arrested for the robbery of the Bisbee Stage. The two men were members of the infamous Cowboys gang in the region. The Earps had the full cooperation of the Cochise County Sheriff's Office, causing a rift between them and the group. Revenge for the arrests was known publicly, but there was not a real indication of the Clantons and McLaurys carrying out their death threats against the Earps.

Soon after, on a Tuesday night, Doc Holliday and Ike Clanton exchanged some nasty words; it was understood that the two men despised each other. The next day, Ike Clanton was arrested by Marshal Virgil Earp for carrying a revolver and rifle, but he was released. He was fined twenty-five dollars by Justice Wallace for carrying concealed weapons.

At that point, Wyatt Earp had heard that Ike Clanton, upon leaving the justice court, had made death threats against him and his brothers and wanted to fight them. Wyatt's response was to state that all he had to do was say how, when and where.

Shortly after that, Billy Clanton and Frank McLaury came into town from Mexico and agreed that a fight would take place. Tom McLaury was in town and had expressed what the residents of Tombstone were already thinking—a fight would hold center stage, and nobody could and would stop them.

Days later, the Cowboys went and looked for Doc Holliday, who was staying at Fly's Boarding House. He wasn't there, but the Earps heard from several people that the Cowboys were at the O.K. Corral spewing threats and hoping that the fight would begin.

It was between 2:00 p.m. and 3:00 p.m. when the Earps went around the corner of Fourth Street and Fremont and headed west to the rear entrance of the O.K. Corral, without hesitation. They met up with the Cowboys in the eighteen-foot-wide alley.

With a cane in his hand, Town Marshal Earp saw the Cowboys place their hands on their gun holsters and said, "Hold on, we don't want that." A pause of the men staring at each other took place for several seconds before guns were drawn. Billy Clanton and Frank McLaury were the first to be shot by Holliday and Morgan Earp.

Billy Clanton drew his gun and began to shoot, while his brother Ike was busy begging Wyatt Earp not to shoot him. At that moment, Morgan Earp and Holliday were focusing on Frank McLaury and Billy Clanton. Frank and Tom McLaury moved their horses to shield them from the flying bullets. Ike Clanton ran away from the gunfight and somehow dodged the slugs from Holliday's gun, while Morgan Earp continued to fire at the now wounded Frank McLaury.

Frank McLaury maneuvered his horse into the street and began shooting as he ducked under the horse's neck. Then, out of nowhere, Holliday pulled out a sawed-off shotgun from under his coat. Even after this explosive gun was shot in his direction, Frank McLaury somehow found a way to hang on to his horse for protection.

Tom McLaury was now shooting over the saddle of his horse and shot Morgan Earp. Immediately, Billy Clanton, who has been seriously wounded, continued to return fire at Virgil and Wyatt Earp. Frank McLaury scored a hit and shot Virgil Earp in the leg.

Morgan Earp was shot through the shoulder muscles and fell to the ground. Tom McLaury's horse was grazed by a shot from Wyatt Earp, leaving the McLaury brother exposed. At this point, Billy Clanton, who was still firing his gun, began to slide down the wall of the Harwood House to the ground.

Tom McLaury, who was mortally wounded, staggered over to the corner of the street and collapsed. The last shot Frank McLaury made hit Holiday's holster, causing a painful but not fatal wound.

Morgan Earp was in serious condition but turned toward Frank McLaury, who was out on Freemont Street, and shot him in the head. Then Earp yelled, "I got him." Frank is dead.

The gunfight at the O.K. Corral lasted about thirty seconds. It was reported that during the gunfight, Sheriff John Behan was nearby shouting for a ceasefire, but he was powerless to stop it.

C.S. Fly's building was right next to the O.K. Corral, and Tom McLaury and Billy Clanton were carried into Fly's Gallery. Tom McLaury died within minutes, but Billy Clanton, who was nineteen years old, died a slow and painful death. Regardless of the large amount of morphine he was administered, witness reported that he was heard yelling and hollering in agony.

The following day, Fly captured an infamous photo of the three dead bodies, posed in black coffins with glass windows, exposing only the head and shoulders of the corpses. Newspapers across the country published the photo. Beneath the men was a sign that read "MURDERED IN THE STREETS OF TOMBSTONE." Hundreds of Tombstone residents followed the Cowboys in a funeral procession to take the three to their final resting place at Boothill Graveyard.

There have been numerous paranormal reports at the infamous grounds of the O.K. Corral, including sightings of ghostly cowboys haunting the infamous site. Footsteps are heard inside and outside the corral and outside area. Disembodied voices also are heard throughout the grounds.

Several reports have been made of seeing Billy Clanton's ghost in that vicinity, which is right on the Fremont Street side of the wall to the O.K. Corral. That's near the location of where the Harwood Building was located and where the Cowboy died. The ghostly sighting at the corner of the intersection might well be Tom McLaury instead, as he is the one who stumbled over to it and fell, after being shot.

There is another ghost haunting the area, with numerous reports of people standing near the O.K. Corral and Tombstone's city park. It's a balding man

O.K. Corral at night, where the ghost of Judge Jim Burnett has been seen. *Author's collection.*

with a long, scrubby beard wearing a black suit. Tourists and locals have seen this man walking or floating almost in the middle of the street and in front of the park, past the O.K. Corral. Without notice, he dissipates into the dark shadows. People have even reported that they've asked this man for directions from afar, in which case the ghost stops, looks directly at them and then vanishes.

There was also a report of a witness, during the late hours of the night, who had heard an odd noise coming out of the O.K. Corral building. He proceeded to take a closer look and stood right in front of the building's window, and to his surprise, he saw a man in a black suit, with balding hair and bushy beard, staring at him with his nose pressed against the window!

After investigating, the witness discovered that there was nobody in the building at that time, as it was closed and locked.

In the Bisbee section of this book, about Evergreen Cemetery, I wrote about Colonel William C. Greene shooting and killing James Burnett, who also went by the title of Justice Jim Burnett. This happened in front of the O.K. Corral. The ghost with a bushy beard and black suit may be Burnett. This is a good place to give the point of view coming from the judge and why his soul may be at unrest.

According to a video by Michael Valenzuela, who claims to be a descendant of Burnett, there was some sort of negotiation that was trying to be reached with Greene. Burnett and the surrounding neighbors were in talks with him regarding water he apparently was damming upstream from his property. Burnett allegedly was willing to pay him for a solution, as the judge needed the water for his cattle.

Burnett and another gentleman named Jeff Hoffman devised a plan to reroute the water through Greene's property and then through the judge's. Valenzuela claimed that before they could finish the project, there was a flash flood that unfortunately took out Greene's dam. This is when Greene's daughter Ella and her friend Katie were swimming in the river; when the dam was destroyed, the girls drowned.

On that dark, gruesome day on July 1, on Allen Street and in front of the O.K. Corral, Burnett was leaving his office. He was checking on a man named Joe Randall, who was in jail for drunkenness. This is when Greene shot the judge and killed him.

Now Burnett's ghost walks up and down the sidewalk in front of the O.K. Corral in a fog of confusion, not quite certain about why he is stuck in his dreadful afterlife. As soon as the slug hit his body, shot by a man on a mission of vengeance, the unexpected blackness he entered must have been a great shock. Is he now mustering a way to prove he wasn't at fault? Burnett is buried at the Tombstone Cemetery.

You might get a chance to ask the ghost if you are visiting the O.K. Corral or walking near it. Good luck.

Boothill Graveyard

There is a place in Cochise County that, because of its perilous record, remains one of the most popular cemeteries to visit in the Wild West. This

Boothill Graveyard is one of the most popular sites to visit on the West Coast. In the 1940s, Emmet Nunnelley was credited to the construction of what is now the cemetery's giftshop. *Author's collection.*

place is the iconic Boothill Graveyard, located in Tombstone. This is where persons of long ago are marked in death as a tribute to their hell-roaring lives spent in a time when life wasn't so easy but is still so romantically and thoroughly studied.

There are approximately 250 markers in the cemetery as reminders of Tombstone's mining heyday, a selection of people who came for a chance at fast money in a variety of ways. Many of the occupants who are memorialized there came to death with their boots on, falling to the explosion of a hot .45-caliber six-shooter slug. Others interred there died as the result of various and poignant incidents that involved men and women murdered in cold blood, men hanged (some legal and others not) and suicide. There are also those who died from natural causes and from a list of bizarre accidents—all are deserving of the enduring memorials instilled in the dirt and rocks at Boothill.

According to a variety of history sources, Boothill was originally given the name of the Tombstone Cemetery and was laid out as a burial plot in 1878. It was used for local pioneers from 1879 to 1884. Before that, people were buried in different locations in town. A new cemetery was created on the west side of the thriving community and is still open. Boothill was then referred to as the "old cemetery" and soon became neglected and overgrown and was

Boothill Graveyard is the last resting place for many criminals and murders, as well as for peaceful souls buried together for eternity. *Randy G. Powers.*

even used as a dumping area. According to "Arizona Death Records Vol. I (A through K): A Bicentennial Project of the Arizona State Genealogical Society," in the late 1920s, a married couple named Emmett and Lela Nunnelley were credited with spearheading a tedious project to restore the graveyard with appropriate markers and historical accuracy to the persons supposedly interred there. It was noted in 1926 in the local newspapers that the Tombstone Boy Scouts were cleaning up the old graveyard, which had been used as a city garbage dump for some time. By 1929, the graveyard had been included in the first celebration of Tombstone's Helldorado Days, a celebration centered on the safeguarding of Tombstone's nefarious history.

By 1937, buying grave markers was at an upmost importance in order to the meet the paucity of tombstones in Boothill. A controversy unfolded during the summer of that same year over the identity of the occupant of a lone iron-fenced grave sitting on a hill in the cemetery.

Emma Smith from St. Joseph, Missouri, carried out a pilgrimage to Tombstone to find her mother Flora Stump's grave. Her investigation led her to the small iron-fenced plot that was a complete mystery to the people of Tombstone. Because of Mrs. Smith's weeklong visit, longtime residents came together to try to remember who was buried there. The article "Boot Hill Brings Order to Buy Grave Markers" in the *Arizona Republic* reported that the *Epitaph*, "Tombstone's only newspaper—entered the argument that was likely because of a shortage of epitaphs—and tombstones—in Tombstone."

After Mrs. Smith left town, letters began pouring in from around the country from sons and daughters of former pioneer residents. With this widespread interest came a great deal of information for the graveyard. A variety of people tried to claim the popular plot, but finally a solid identification was made. This grave site did indeed belong to Flora Stump. A woman named Bertha Strinker said that her mother had brought her there before and told her that her Aunt Flora was buried there. She said Flora was pregnant at the time of her death, and two weeks before her due date, she became very ill with a toothache. A dentist in town decided to extract the bad tooth and administered chloroform as the anesthetic. Apparently, it was an overdose, and Flora never regained consciousness.

Strinker said, "Joe Stump, my uncle, buried her and, as a symbol of his affection, marked her grave with an iron fence. He returned to Missouri with his daughter Emma and son Frank with him, to the place where the journey to Tombstone started, for he lived there before starting West." Strinker's story was accepted by the Tombstone Chamber of Commerce.

It seems that there were several occurrences that created the Boothill Graveyard. By the 1940s, Emmet Nunnelley was heavily involved with the construction of the building what is now the cemetery's gift shop and took over the management.

According to a pamphlet created by Lela Nunnelley in 1962, many of the 250 graves have unidentified markers. The information includes tragic deaths. The earliest burial was a one-year-old girl named Agnes Kenny in

1878. According to the pamphlet, she was given calomel, which was used for teething in a powder form, but unfortunately it contains mercury. She died shortly after the local doctor gave it to her.

The last person buried there was a man named Glenn Will, who had the nickname of "Bronco Bill." He was raised in Tombstone and moved elsewhere. Will expressed to his son that he always wanted to return one day to his hometown. So, when he died, his son sent his cremated ashes C.O.D., and he became the last person to be buried there in 1953.

Of course, Boothill has markers dedicated to the participants of the gunfight in 1881 at the O.K. Corral. This includes Tom and Frank McLaury and Billy Clanton. There is a large plot with a marker reading, "Murdered in the streets of Tombstone."

Another notable set of graves belongs to the men who were the killers at the Bisbee Massacre in 1883. Dan Dowd, Red Sample, Tex Howard, Bill Delaney and Dan Kelly share a marker with "Legally Hanged, March 25th, 1884."

John Heath has his own marker that reads, "John Heath taken from County Jail & LYNCHED by Bisbee Mob in Tombstone, February 22, 1884." His body was later removed, and he was buried in Terrell, Texas.

One of the more famous markers in Boothill Graveyard reads, "Here Lies Lester Moore Four Slugs from a 44. No Les. No More."

With the unfortunate history of the people who were interred here, it's not a surprise that there would be a heavy dose of paranormal activity recorded. Also, the redesign of the cemetery over the years may have something to with some of the supernatural disturbances documented on the property. The graveyard grounds experienced different types of havoc, including how Highway 80 was constructed through Tombstone in the early 1930s. The new road split the land of the cemetery, causing some of the bodies to be moved to the other town cemetery. Also, houses and different types of buildings were built over the area of the old graveyard. Because of these and other reasons, the dead are showing themselves in different ways. The City of Tombstone owns the graveyard as of May 2019 and now leases it to the Tombstone Chamber of Commerce.

Wayne Sorenson is a former Boothill gift shop manager and told me that the graveyard has a lot of paranormal activity reported by employees and visitors. One of the incredible events Sorenson mentioned was that when they were clearing for the old Circle K store a block or so away, two bodies were discovered. This matches with the history of people buried in different areas of Tombstone before Boothill Graveyard was created.

Sorenson also described how a little girl no older than five came up to the counter of the gift shop and said, "There's a little boy out there and he wanted to play, but then he disappeared." Sorenson said that she was the sweetest child and didn't seem to be scared. Her parents said they didn't see anything but that she wouldn't lie about something like that and added that their child repeated herself about what she saw.

A medium told the store manager that there was an old man spirit named Kevin who is in the building, and when the children play with the magnetic rocks they have for sale and make noise, it makes him mad.

Employees have reported that when they would open the doors first thing in the morning, Wyatt Earp books would be on the floor—only Earp books. I asked if it could be the spirit of Billy Clanton since he is interred in the cemetery. Sorensen said that it could be him or the McLaury brothers.

Another supernatural incident took place in the shop when some Native American dolls sitting on a shelf, next to another set with a space gap of about five feet, physically moved or jumped off and landed on the floor by themselves. Two employees witnessed this. They told Sorensen, and he said he took the information and went on with his day. Then, later that same day, an elderly woman came out of the bathroom, went right up to him and said, "Sir, there's an Indian chief sitting on the floor in one of the stalls." This happened around 2017.

Sorenson said that he was a sceptic about ghosts until the day he decided to use a ghost app on his phone. As he sat at his register with the app on, five words came up on his phone. They included *rage*, *bed*, *bottom* and *flow*, which he interpreted as the description for a river. Then the last word struck him with astonishment. It was the name Brady.

There are two graves of brothers who drowned in the San Pedro River in 1883 during monsoon season. The brothers were John, age eleven, and Frank, age twelve. While one was drowning, the other brother died in a vain attempt to save his brother. Sorenson said that after that experience, he became a believer.

According to various newspaper article reports, the brothers were Tombstone residents and nephews of Carr Stephenson, the owner of the Last Chance Saloon. They were with several other children at a very popular swimming spot on the river. When the drowning incident took place, the other children made a run for help from anyone in nearby Charleston and notified Owen McDernott. Regardless of people attempting to save them, the boys drowned.

Along with my husband, Randy; daughter Brittany; son Grant (Randy G.); and grandson Andre, we were granted the privilege to do a paranormal

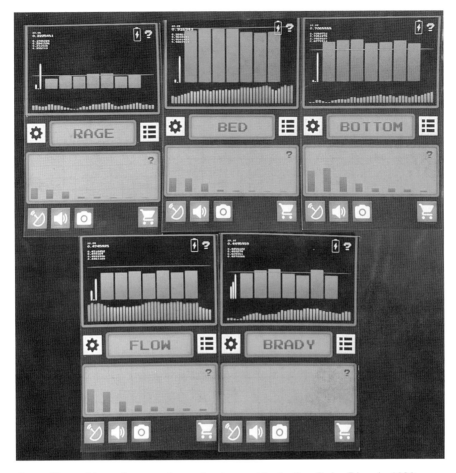

Compelling evidence from two boys who drowned in the San Pedro River in 1883. *Wayne Sorenson.*

investigation after hours at Boothill Graveyard. During the investigation, photos, EVPs (electronic voice phenomena) and EMF (electromagnetic field) levels were taken at particular graves, and pictures were also taken throughout the cemetery.

The first grave site I headed for, because of Sorenson's experience, was of the two Brady brothers. An EVP of a young boy was recorded. As I stood over the double plot, I asked a slew of questions, and as I spoke, I picked up on one of the spirits saying, "I grabbed his hair." I was also connecting to the spirit lying on the left side facing the entire graveyard and got chills. At that time on the voice recorder, the disembodied voice said, "Make him kick off."

Left: John Brady Jr. *Boothill Cemetery.*

Below: Francine Powers at the Brady brothers' grave site during her EVP session with the boys. *Brittany Maklary.*

Brittany was standing with me, but as soon as my son and grandson walked up to where we were standing, I felt a sense of excitement from the spirit. At the end of this session, I asked the spirit to make a sound or talk into the object I was holding. There were two hard taps and then two more ending with one hard tap at the end of the recording. I did not touch or hit my recorder in that way whatsoever. I'm not sure what the message from one of the boys was trying to convey to me or if it was his way of just saying that he was listening and acknowledging my presence.

We moved on to the grave of Red Sample, who was one of those hanged at the gallows of the Tombstone Courthouse due to his contribution to the killings at the Bisbee Massacre. As a group, we all bantered with the man in the grave, with a much different tone and attitude compared to the Brady brothers. As we spoke, my recorder seemed to continuously shut off on its own, making me restart many times. As soon as we mentioned that we were from Bisbee, the EMF detector began to light up, especially when we mentioned Mrs. Roberts, the pregnant woman who was shot and killed during the massacre.

My grandson Andre continuously told Sample to make the EMF go to orange, and the spirit obliged and responded very well to the mention of the gallows. Sample seemed very agitated. When we decided to leave his grave, I said to him, "You *have* to stay here. You do not have permission to follow us. Stay here." The EMF completely lit up. The spirit was extremely unsettled at this remark. There were no EVPs or oddities in any photographs taken there.

At the plot of the three men who were killed during the O.K. Corral shootout, several pieces of paranormal activity were felt and reordered. I spoke to the three men buried there, and after a few moments, my daughter and I began to experience chills and goosebumps. I also felt intimidated and a deep fog of hatred and anger seemed to hover over us, expelled from the spirits presenting themselves as I spoke.

Tom McLaury was the first I communicated with, and I told him directly that he was shot and killed over on Freemont and Third Street. Did he remember? I also said that people have seen Billy Clanton's ghost near the same place. I asked if that were true, and on my recording, he responded at that moment with a ghostly laugh. At that time, my daughter was restating that she had the chills and that they were intensifying.

I then began to fell a heavy presence and asked who was there. At that point on the recording, you can hear birds singing very faintly and then a lone human whistle. A disembodied voice says, "Sing." The EVP was very clear and sounded like the voice was from a young man.

Grave site for the infamous men who died at the gunfight at the OK Corral. *Randy G. Powers.*

A few moments after that, I began to feel as if I was going to be slapped. I felt the negative energy coming from the direction of Frank McLaury. As I was deciphering that feeling, my husband, son and grandson walked up to the large plot. My grandson brought up the movie *Tombstone* and asked who the guy was who seemed to wear a red shirt all the time. Randy said his name was "Curly Bill" Brocius. As soon as those words were spoken, the EMF meter lit up like a Christmas tree.

I asked the spirit, "You recognized the name Curly Bill?" Because the meter was lying directly over the space for Tom McLaury, I said, "Curly Bill died, Tom." Brittany added, "Just like you." Immediately, the EMF meter went off again. We gasped. After that, all we had to do was mention Curly Bill for the EMF lights to roll up and down.

We moved the meter to the grave of Frank McLaury, and when Andre told him, "You should've made your shots," the EMF meter flashed. When it was moved over to Billy's grave, he reacted the same way.

Those who are interred here are visited by people across the world, intrigued with those whose last place on earth is at the top of Boothill. From that mount, the old ghosts of Tombstone hear strangers talk about them and their own lives and deaths. As we visit those graves, we can hope that the people buried there have peace and finally walk off into the Arizona sunset, away from the fiery heat of the hard life of the young western frontier they call Cochise County.

THE BRUNCKOW CABIN

One of the haunted sites I covered in my online magazine *Spirits of Cochise County* was the Brunckow Cabin. Following is the article in its entirety.

On top of a small hill in the thick of the Arizona desert sits a few falling walls. If they could talk, they would tell you stories filled with terror, violence, gore and pure madness. This very spot is where historians say twenty people have been murdered, including the very people who built it. The Brunckow Cabin has the nickname of the "Bloodiest Cabin in Arizona."

Brunckow Cabin ruins. *Author's collection.*

Frederick Brunckow, a German mining engineer, built the cabin in 1858 as he worked on nearby claims. He worked for a regional mining company and established a claim in the 1850s that was located a few miles from where Tombstone is now.

Brunckow had a small team to begin his mining business. According to the book *Weird Arizona: Your Travel Guide to Arizona's Legends and Best Kept Secrets*, Brunckow had a chemist with him, a cook named David Brontrager and two other miners who were cousins, James and William Williams. Brunckow hired Mexican laborers to assist with building the living quarters and a supply store. It took two years before they were ready to begin drilling for ore in 1860.

In the hot month of July, William Williams had to make a supply run to nearby Fort Buchanan. He was gone for several days, and upon his return, during the blackness of the night, he found a shocking spectacle of savagery and horror.

As William jumped off his now packed wagon, he took his lantern and shined it on the small building that Brunckow and his laborers had constructed, only to find it completely torn apart. He soon found his cousin James dead, with his body already decaying. Immediately, William left the scene to head back to Fort Buchanan to get help. Soldiers from the U.S. Army followed William back and almost immediately found the dead body of the team's chemist outside the cabin. The body had been scavenged by animals of the desert. They also found the body of Brunckow in a shaft near the cabin. The miner had been horrifically killed by impalement with a rock drill. The soldiers buried the bodies near the cabin.

Brontrager, the camp cook, showed up the next day. He told William and the soldiers that he had been hiding out in the desert for four days. Brontrager said that only a few hours after William left, the laborers attacked a wagon that had brought a supply of goods. The cook said the Mexicans stole money and horses after they violently killed the three men. Unfortunately, the Mexican men were never found and were never tried for the coldblooded murders.

Within twenty years of the triple murder at the cabin, seventeen more deaths took place on the same spot. Because there was a good water supply with a wide wash directly below the cabin, people kept coming back to move in, but instead they were met by the grim reaper himself.

According to historians, the cabin was vacant for many years before the first U.S. marshal of the Arizona Territory, named Major Milton B. Duffield, decided to move in. Unfortunately, Duffield was also a victim of the cabin's curse and was also murdered.

The cabin's ruins are located near Tombstone and, appropriately enough, on Brunckow Road. There is a small hike of about six hundred meters from the dirt road. My husband, Randy, and I went to investigate the historical site and began to walk through the rocky and rough trail at sunset to the Brunckow Cabin to find out if this spot would live up to its haunted reputation.

As we hiked the trail leading directly to the ruins, the sun began to fall behind the mountains. The walk didn't seem to take long, as we gained excitement for the investigation with each step. Along the trail and on the left side going west toward the San Pedro River, we heard an odd wailing in the distance. We stopped a few times to make sure it wasn't coyotes or another wild animal. It sounded more human than animal. This gave off an eerie sensation as we neared the cabin.

As we walked over a small mound of rock and sand near the end of the narrow trail, we could see the Brunckow Cabin across the wide sandy wash, tucked in a group of mesquite bushes atop of a small hill. The shadows of the ruins had a strange yet attractive look to it as it took in the last sun rays of the day.

We began to take pictures of the ruins from all angles, hoping to surprise any spirits that may be there. I turned on my digital recorder and left it on the entire investigation. We calmly walked around the cabin, focusing on any sensations. I approached what looked like the doorway to the building, introduced myself and asked any spirit there a series of questions directed toward the history of the cabin. I asked if anyone was buried near the structure and, if so, please throw a rock in the direction of its grave.

I didn't have to wait longer than a few seconds before we could hear a rock hitting the ground toward the back of the cabin. Randy went in the direction of where the rock landed. Then he pointed his flashlight toward me to signal me over to where he was standing. He said, "Look at that. This is odd."

Directly behind the ruins were two pieces of rebar lying on the ground in the shape of a cross. Another group of visitors may have left this here in honor of those who lost their lives, but the sequence of events leading up to its find seemed interestingly coincidental.

The name James came into my mind as we stood behind the cabin, but as soon as we decided to move to another location, the name seemed to fade. We decided to go into the center of the ruins, and before crossing the doorway, we asked if we could come in. At the doorway and before entering, I had a heavy and smothering impression along with a feeling of dread.

To encourage the spirit's participation, a lantern was set on the ground with a twig balancing on a small rock so the entity or entities could move it. After a few seconds, we got a creepy surprise when a large black widow crawled over the twig instead.

After that, we decided to do an EVP session outside the cabin. I personally began to feel the sensation of a dark and tall figure clinging behind me. We asked the spirit or spirits to present answers. I asked the spirit if it realized he was dead and, if so, was he shot to death? An EVP of a disembodied voice replied with "Yes."

Unfortunately, since Charleston Road is positioned so close to the Brunckow Cabin, the sound of traffic drowned out anything else that may have been captured and presented as evidence. The EVP session was cut short, as we felt too uncomfortable to go on with the investigation. We gathered our things and left the historical site.

I was able to capture many glowing orbs in and around the cabin, and Randy and I concluded that the site of the Brunckow Cabin has a dark, magnetic power that projects doom and fear. Whatever source of evil has implanted itself there may be the reason why this site could be the most violent spot of ground in Arizona.

DOUGLAS

In 1905, the Calumet and Arizona Mining Company, which was operating the mega-mines in nearby Bisbee, created the city of Douglas, Arizona. The mining giants had to address the heavy smoke coming from the plumes of the smelters located directly in the middle of the city of Bisbee. They decided to purchase a great deal of land near the international border of the United States and Mexico, about twenty-five miles southeast of Bisbee.

With the El Paso and Southwestern Railroad and the new property for the smelter operation, mining transportation for the large amounts of ore excavated became uncomplicated for the local industry. The ore was transported to various locations internationally and across the country from Bisbee to Douglas and then out to the world. The new smelters were set at a site near but still outside of a community that had a carefully engineered layout and was named after one of the most famous mining pioneers, Dr. James Douglas.

Douglas, Arizona, has a population of about 16,500 residents and has been called one of the nation's top micropolitan area. This includes communities with 10,000 to 50,000 residents, with rising economies, exceptional amenities and moderate costs of living.

GADSDEN HOTEL

In the town of Douglas, there is a grand building that hovers over the city landscape. This landmark was built around the time the smelter town was just created and incorporated. The Gadsden Hotel was opened in 1907 and named after the Gadsden Purchase. A fantastic group of businessmen and millionaire mining investors got together as the Gadsden Company, later renamed the Douglas Investment Company. The members of this powerful group were John Slaughter, Lem Shattuck, Mike Cunningham and Dr. James Douglas.

The hotel was built in about one year, and the plans were originally made by Trost and Trost of El Paso, with the construction contract given to Otto Krueuger. The hotel was a luxurious place and could accommodate mining officials, businessmen, politicians and military personnel who traveled to Douglas for a variety of reasons. The building was also a place for ranchers and farmers, with families in tow, to shop and do some serious cattle negotiations. There have always been many office spaces in the hotel used by several different types of businesses and organizations.

The *Douglas Dispatch* reported that opening-day events at the hotel took place on Thanksgiving Day and included an elegant party with dancing and fine food. The lobby was filled with leather chairs and matching rugs in the center of the very large room. A dining room, saloon, barbershop and a men's clothing store all adjoined the foyer. At the time of the Gadsden's opening, the rooms were rented for $1.50 and $2.00 per night.

It was reported that in 1915, during the same three-day siege by Pancho Villa on the Mexican border town of Aqua Prieta and the same battles mentioned earlier, buildings shook in Douglas. There were shots from cannons and machine gun fire just across the border. People who lived in Douglas and the surrounding areas were known to go up on the roof of the hotel to watch. During one of those viewing events, a stray shot from a battle hit the elevator shaft behind a crowd of onlookers, forcing them inside.

The Gadsden Hotel survived Prohibition and was favored for its location close to the international border. Guests only had to either walk or drive a short distance to cross over to a location unaffected by Prohibition.

On February 7, 1928, the entire building block became engulfed in flames at the loss of approximately $200,000. The entire hotel structure was destroyed. According to the *Douglas Daily Dispatch*, guests were safely evacuated from the burning building before the walls started caving in. Volunteers assisted from nearby restaurants and businesses. A woman was

The opulent lobby of the Gadsden Hotel is not only stunning to look at but gives a haunting impression as well. *Tanya Duarte.*

reportedly carried from the burning inferno. The hotel was completely gutted from the attic to the basement, and all the businesses occupying the building were destroyed or rendered unsalvageable. The only things left were the elevator car cabin, the marble staircase and marble columns.

The fire alarm sounded at about 5:12 a.m., but the fire started close to twenty minutes before that. All the firemen from the fire department were there—all ten of them. Chief William J. Nemeck, along with about twelve volunteers, tried to fight the fire with four streams of water but were unsuccessful. Witnesses there said that it wouldn't have mattered if six fire departments were there—the hotel still would've burned to the ground. The hotel was immediately rebuilt with the same architect and a limitless budget.

Now the Gadsden Hotel is five stories, four above ground and a basement. It was rebuilt as a safe and fireproof building. There is a grand stained-glass window that stretches across the east side of the lobby. The window and two large skylights were made created by Ralph Baker. Underneath the stained-glass mural is an oil-painting titled *Cave Creek Canyon* by artist Audley Dean

Nichols. There are amber-colored marble columns and $7,000 (at time of construction) worth of gold leaf used to decorate the inset panels around the columns and skylights.

There is a mezzanine that forms a balcony that extends three sides of the lobby and ends with two marble stairways that are wonderfully placed under the large window. There are twin statues of Spanish conquistadores on the pedestals at the bottom of the curved staircase. The Gadsden holds the rights to the infamous story of Pancho Villa. He supposedly rode his steed Siete Leguas into the hotel lobby with both six-shooters firing as he raced up and down the marbled staircase, screaming words of war and freedom. Storytellers say that he left a chip on the marbled staircase. Another story included a rodeo clown who rode a trained bull through the lobby and into the saloon.

The Gadsden Hotel has 160 rooms; was the first hotel to have individual bathrooms in each room, with air-cooled rooms; and had the first telephone switchboard of its kind in Arizona in 1929. The hotel was also the backdrop for numerous movies, TV shows and videos. It has been renovated over the decades. Some famous guests have included John Dillinger, Charlie Sheen, Nastassja Kinski, NFL quarterback Mike Pagel and countless other diplomats, movie and television stars and various celebrities.

This building is also a magnet to many psychics, who come to communicate with several entities inhabiting the hotel. Past hotel manager Robin Brekhus has been quoted saying that most incidents happen during the Christmas season.

I wrote about the hauntings at the hotel in my 2004 book, *Mi Reina: Don't Be Afraid*, noting that various occurrences tied to unexplainable events have played out in the ancient building. Hotel maids over the years have alleged to have been slapped in the face by an invisible attacker, doors open and slam shut by themselves and muffled cries and shrieks come from empty rooms—all documented incidents from many visitors over decades of public usage.

During 1987, while I was working as a hostess for the hotel's restaurant, I was asked to help one of the busboys. He was assigned room service duty, and due to a rush of customers, I was delivering a lunch tray to a room on the third floor. As I waited for the hotel guest to answer my knock, I began to feel uneasy standing alone in the long hall by myself. Suddenly, something whispered "hey…hey" through the corridor. I immediately looked around and saw no one. I knocked again. The whispering voice repeated the same words. This time, I turned completely in a circle looking for who was there and said out loud, "Hello? Who's there?" At that moment, I heard footsteps approaching me, but there was nobody there. I repeated myself out loud again, "Who's there?"

My arms and legs began to tremble. I turned around and began to knock harder at the door and hollered, "Lunch!" I didn't want to turn around again, too scared of what was coming my way. The hall became incredibly cold. The floor seemed to vibrate as the voice of the invisible entity repeated its words. Then, suddenly, the door opened wide, with a woman offering an apology for taking so long and explaining that she was in the shower. She took the tray, and I left the hallway with more speed than I have ever mastered. Not until I landed on the first floor again did I feel at ease.

Tanya Duarte was a manager at the Gadsden for three years and told me that she had experienced many events that she can attribute to being spiritual in nature. Here is her testimony about the paranormal activity she has experienced, in her own words:

> One of the most well-known at the hotel is a young boy. He is impish, like a little brother who likes to tease people. He was one that we would often see out of the corner of our eye wandering around the mezzanine level. Where he would be, things often went missing such as keys, rings, and other small items. They would often be found quite a bit later in very obscure locations. People would also report that they would feel their clothes or their hair being tugged on, and the TV or AC in their rooms turning off and on. One fun story involving him was a guest that was in one of the rooms with her husband one night. While she was asleep, she sensed someone watching her. She knew that no one was there, and she picked up her phone and started taking pictures in the dark. Upon looking at the pictures the little boy could be seen clearly. I asked her to send me the pictures while she was right in front of me. She sent them to my phone; the picture came but the little boy was not in it. I asked her to email it to me, she did. The picture came, again the little boy was not in the image. As a last-ditch effort, I used my phone to take a picture of her phone. Again, the little boy did not show in the picture. He only showed in the pictures on her phone, nowhere else.
>
> Also, at the Gadsden we experienced other entities. We could hear people talking in areas that there were no people. We could smell cigar smoke and perfume where there were no people. There was always a feeling that someone was there even when there wasn't. When we would do things as such as construction and remodeling in the building, we could feel the energy shift; sometimes it felt angry, sometimes it felt happy,

most often it felt judgmental. We knew that we were visiting and making changes in their home. We could only hope that they approved. At times they did not, and we could feel the negativity permeating the walls. It was a feeling as if we knew we were in trouble for doing the wrong thing.

One time, I left late in the evening. The only one there was our security personnel. We were in the middle of renovating the restaurant. We completely gutted it to start all over making a beautiful new restaurant. That night when I left, everything was in place, clean and looking beautiful. When I returned in the morning, I noticed that every wall sconce in the lobby had been angled in different directions. I asked the security gentleman and he had not even noticed. When I went to move them to the proper angle, every single one was tight. I had to get the screwdriver to loosen them so that I could properly position them. There was no explanation on why they had been moved or how. The security footage showed nothing, one minute they were proper, the next they were angled. Things like that happened frequently. We just accepted it.

The third floor of the Gadsden hotel is where one can sense the most energies. For those who are very sensitive, especially children, it could be quite scary. However, there was never a sense that these spirits were evil or revengeful. It was just like you are visiting a stranger's home. Sometimes that person might just be grouchy or in a bad mood. Sometimes we would feel as if it was the old man yelling at us to get off his lawn. After leaving the third floor it was important to follow a certain protocol so as not to bring that energy to other areas.

The basement is a location where everyone would think the darkest spirits would reside. At the Gadsden hotel that was not the case. The feeling in the basement was one of fun and frolicking happiness. We could see many orbs floating around. On the surveillance videos you could see orbs following people around the basement. They flittered around like a field of butterflies. It was almost as if you could feel the giggling. Later, I had been told a story that in this area during prohibition there was a popular drink that was served in the Speakeasy in the basement that was called "Giggle Juice." It seems as if that party continues.

One more world-renowned story that is attached to the Gadsden includes Pancho Villa. A headless apparition has been seen over the years at the hotel, and it might well be his ghost. It is said that Villa tattooed the map of hidden money or some other kind of treasure on his head. When he was killed in 1923, rumors spread saying that grave robbers took his head and hid it in the basement of the Gadsden Hotel. People say that the spirit is Villa looking for his head. While others say it's a past owner of the Gadsden from the 1930s who knew about the legendary story and spent all his life looking for Villa's head and is still searching after his own death. Others claim that Villa's head is in a frat house in a safe at Harvard University.

AVENUE HOTEL

There is a place in Douglas, Arizona, filled with captivating history and mystery that includes the true-life story of a young mother whose death was ruled as a suicide, but the circumstances remain cryptic. The Avenue Hotel originally opened in 1901 as the Railroad Hotel. It was frequently used by railroad workers and other travelers. The original building is made from adobe and was constructed by the Douglas Land and Improvement Company. In 1915, the hotel was expanded, and the new addition was made of brick. The Avenue Hotel was run by the Bruno family since the 1920s until it closed in 1973, when the El Paso and Southwestern Railroad shut down that same year. Robin Brekhus has owned Avenue Hotel since 2007.

Brekhus officially opened her hotel in 2013. She is originally from North Dakota and spends her summers as an event coordinator for an air museum, but she has been a Douglas resident for decades. She ran the Gadsden Hotel for her father-in-law for nearly twenty-five years, starting in 1988.

I interviewed Brekhus, and she said that Rose Bruno owned the business; she thinks that the majority of her clientele was from the railroad. Rose Bruno lived there until she died in 1986. At that point, Frank Bruno, her son, moved in. Brekhus met Frank, as he was a regular at the Gadsden's restaurant. Brekhus said the two became close friends, and even after she bought the hotel from him, they stayed in close contact and had lunch when they could. Frank Bruno just recently died at the age of ninety-five. He was an acquaintance of mine, as I knew him from my time working at the Gadsden as well. He was very passionate about his hotel and spoke about restoring it.

"Frank made sure I got the hotel; they were selling it for twice the amount I paid. It was meant for me. And he knew it," stated Brekhus.

The original side of the hotel was built in a shotgun style and is only twenty-five feet wide, with rooms on each side of the hall upstairs. The

Avenue Hotel in Douglas, Arizona. *Robin Brekhus.*

older side had no heat or running water, and guests would have to use an outhouse back in the early 1900s. Of course, now Avenue Hotel has all the modern amenities. The hotel has fifteen rooms, varying in sizes from suites and double and single bedrooms and studio apartments. There is a barber/dentist office with original late 1800s inventory. Items such as straight razors, medicine bottles and tonics give the room a movie set ambiance.

There is also an upstairs poker room, overlooking the Mabel Magee's Old West dining room. This part of the hotel is for diners with reservations and is a destination for parties and special occasions.

When asked about the paranormal activity at the hotel, Brekhus was very forthcoming in her information. She said, "So, Mabel is one of my ghosts. Her room is number 20, where she died in 1905. The other ghost is a man named David." She stated that David was her bookkeeper when she was running the Gadsden and was fired by the new management. Sadly, he eventually became homeless and then very ill. Brekhus said that David moved into her hotel and died there not too long ago.

"I got a bench in the backyard with a plaque in honor of him. David is around. My dogs even see him sometimes. We see him and feel him too at times," stated Brekhus. She added, "After David died, the whole hotel was going crazy with ghosts. We saw David everywhere. I think he shook up all the ghosts at the hotel." She also said that David used to smoke and sit at a large swing outside on the patio. It was a two-seater, and her dog Rylie would sit opposite of David often. To this day, Brekhus said that her dog will sit where she used to and stare at where David used to sit.

The hotel owner said that when Frank Bruno was living there, he called the police several times. She said he lived there by himself and would hear odd noises and people walking in the building. The police would come and investigate, and they would hear different things and footsteps but never found anyone else in the hotel.

"Frank installed a window in room seven, which was his living space and the same room he grew up in. He also put in a two-way mirror so he could see all the way down the hall to catch if anyone was sneaking up on him," stated Brekhus. He also shared with Brekhus that the hotel was haunted by the ghost of Mabel, an eighteen-year-old waitress and maid at the hotel. She was a mother to a two-year-old and was reported to have committed suicide by drinking a large amount of morphine.

According to a 1905 article in the *Bisbee Daily Review* titled "Woman Attempts Suicide at Douglas," Mabel was married to Frank Farrell, and at the

A haunted patio swing at the Avenue Hotel. *Robin Brekhus.*

time of that publication, she was at the point of death and still at the Avenue Hotel. This being the result of a supposed self-administration of poison. It was reported that the hotel's manager, Mrs. Marksbury, went upstairs on March 12 to get Mabel to wait on tables, but she received no answer from the girl's room. The door was forced open, and the manager found Mabel lying on the bed unconscious. A doctor was immediately summoned, and every effort was made to wake her up. At this point, the doctor wasn't sure if the young woman could be saved.

Mable was very well liked and seemingly happy, yet it was believed that she had attempted to kill herself. Another article the same week noted that the woman had died on March 15 as the result of an overdose of morphine. The article, "Douglas Woman Dead from Morphine Poisoning by Her Own Hand," stated that unfinished notes found in her room supposedly indicated the reason she might have taken her own life. The notes suggested that the cause of the rash act was a disappointment in a love affair.

Mabel's maiden name was Cavenas, and she was from Naco, Arizona. She married a Mexican bullfighter named Alfonso Armenta at the young age of thirteen. He deserted her soon after. She moved to Douglas but soon met and moved in with Farrell. It was reported that Farrell left for El Paso four months before Mabel's death.

Mable had just started her job at the hotel two months prior, and according to employees there, she was a very good worker, cheerful and popular. Her suicide was completely unexpected and a shock to anyone who knew her or crossed paths. Because of other circumstances that Brekhus shared and her own research into Mable's mysterious death, it is questionable whether it was suicide or murder. Brekhus said, "I have a judge's inquest from a trial held to determine if the death of Mabel was suicide or foul play."

It was testified that Frank abused Mabel, and there were many witnesses to the violence. A young man named Charles Dahlquist was living down the hall from the young woman at the time. He was an electrician at the Copper Queen smelter as a crane man and had witnessed Frank trying to strangle Mable. Another person saw Frank slapping her. Brekhus stated, "Frank comes to the hotel and the couple have a big fight. He threatens to kill her if she doesn't come with him. She doesn't want to go. He leaves."

The story continued with a woman named Mrs. Stevens, who lived across the hall from Mabel. She heard the couple fight, and after Frank left, she went to Mabel and invited her to go to a saloon next door to have a few drinks. Later, the bartender testified that Mabel had two or three beers, nothing unusual for the young woman. After the drinks, the bartender said that suddenly Mabel couldn't walk and acted woozy. She was so unstable that the bartender and Mrs. Stevenson helped take the eighteen-year-old to her room.

They laid her down, and both became so worried about her condition that they called a local doctor, who found that she had taken too much morphine. Unfortunately, Mable never regained consciousness.

"I think Frank gave her the morphine. He had just seen her before she went to the saloon," stated Brekhus. She added, "Suicide notes were found in her room. There are three. One is illegible; the second one says, 'My darling Mr. Dahlquist. I have taken morphine and I don't expect to live.' The last one says, 'Momma, please don't let them put me underground unless you know I am truly dead.'"

Brekhus said that the notes were on Avenue Hotel stationery from 1905. "Frank was in and out of the hotel and could've gotten the stationery easily," stated Brekhus. She also thinks that Frank was jealous of Dahlquist. During the trial, it was also noted that Mabel turned nervous and scared when Frank entered a room.

Dahlquist also testified in court that he had a small supply of morphine and so did Mrs. Stevenson. While Mabel lay in bed dying, they both checked their rooms to see if she may have taken their supply. They both said that their morphine supplies were still present.

During this time, Brekhus said that opium and laudanum were easily obtained in Douglas. Laudanum was opiates mixed with alcohol and was often prescribed for an array of aches and pains. This was also very addicting and was often used to commit suicide.

The hotel owner shared how some extraordinary paranormal activity happened in the Avenue kitchen and dining room before it opened for business. Her best friend, Kelly, asked if Brekhus would allow another business owner who owned a ranch in Douglas to have a meeting in the bar and restaurant area of the hotel. The meeting was over the maintenance of a road that the rancher sold and concerned who would be maintaining it as it still went through some of his property.

Brekhus agreed and had a group of five or six people painting in various rooms in the hotel at the same time of the meeting. During this time, a loud crash was heard coming out of the kitchen. "There is a shelf above my stove, and it had a large stack of plates on it. When I heard the crash, I ran to the kitchen and saw the plates broken everywhere. I asked Mabel if she was mad that I was opening the hotel soon. A little time after, Kelly came in and said she had to leave and asked if it was okay if the two men continued their

Left: Room 20, where the young woman named Mabel died. *Robin Brekhus.*

Right: Robin Brekhus, Avenue Hotel owner. *Robin Brekhus.*

meeting," stated Brekhus. She then asked Kelly if she heard the crash. Kelly said she'd call later.

Later in the day, Kelly called Brekhus to say that she was in agreement and thought that it was Mabel the ghost who caused the plates to be pushed off the shelf. She told Brekhus that at the moment of the crash, the two men were in a very heated argument; both were half standing up from their chairs, and each had a hand on his sidearm.

Kelly said, "There was nothing I could do to quiet them down. Then, as soon as the crash in the kitchen happened, it changed everything. The two men calmed down and sat down. I felt confident enough to leave them alone. As I left, they were making deals on how much the rancher was going to get paid to maintain the road." A side note is that the table they were using is directly below Mabel's room in the hotel.

Brekhus said that anytime anyone is acting loud or a little ruthless at the hotel, Mabel will knock over a lamp or turn on a light, seemingly to snap the person out of their anger or maybe even to give a warning for them to stop. "The time the plates were pushed off the shelf and made the big crash was a big one—I believe Mabel was doing just that," said Brekhus.

LA LLORONA

Various cultures have eerie stories that are passed from generation to generation. One is the story of La Llorona ("the weeping one"), from Latin America, more directly from Mexico. In my first book about ghosts in the region, I mentioned my encounter with the entity on Twelfth Street in Douglas in 1994. Here is the excerpt from my book, *Mi Reina*:

This story includes the record of a tormented soul of a mother of five small children, who was a wife to an unfaithful man. The husband was well-known and liked, whom during one rain filled night, was found in the arms of another woman. After searching for him because he hadn't been home for days, at a local drinkery, she found her husband wrapped in the lust of a stranger. The wife went completely insane. Her actions were astonishing. Instead of attacking the adulterers, she chose to turn from the scene and run home.

As the broken woman entered her tiny shack, she began to wail uncontrollably, turning every piece of furniture upside down. She screamed profanities as she tore the sleeves of her worn blouse, and then threw her thin wedding band into the fireplace. She kicked over the hurricane lamp on the dining room table, causing a burst of flames to erupt and flash in the middle of the small room.

Then she suddenly stopped and stood frozen. She began to take in long, penetrating deep breaths as she held her hands into tight fists on either side of her hips. The woman then fell to the ground and began to hit the wooden floor with her balled up hands, shaking her long, coarse grey hair into a whirlwind of rage. She stopped her tantrum, then slowly brought herself up from the floor. Standing, she turned her red-faced and glossed-over eyes toward her trembling children, who were huddled up together in a corner of the room.

At this point, the small fire started by the overturned lamp, was growing higher. The woman didn't take notice. She instead let out a long and demonic scream, then started to grab and holler at her children while she slapped and pulled at their arms and hair.

Falling to the ground in pure exhaustion, she began to mumble strange words in a whisper as her eyes rolled back. As the small home began to fill with smoke, she crawled on her knees over to her white shawl on the floor. She grabbed it then gently put it over her head, letting it drape down to her waist. She stood up, then ordered her children to follow her outside. Once the smallest child was out, she jerked him by his left arm and threatened to break his neck if the rest didn't follow.

She dragged them all to the raging river near the house. As a thunderstorm terrorized the dark night with heavy rain and blinding lightning strikes, the enraged woman began to do the unspeakable. She threw each babe into the freezing cold water, screaming and crying the entire time. The family home burned in an inferno, in the background.

After the horrific deed was finished, she instantly snapped out of her psychotic rage, and realized what she had done. She watched helplessly on the bank from above, as her children began to drown. They called to her begging for her rescue, until finally the woman watched her children's limp bodies float down the river, dead.

Now, with absolutely nothing to live for, she too, threw herself into the same fatal water. Thus, ending the night of terror with silence.

Now, that spirit of La Llorona travels the desert looking for the children she murdered. She wails and screams in pain. The night wind carries her mournful cries across the washes, ditches, alleys of towns and cities. The sad entity glides low and close to the ground. Trying to catch a glimpse of a child, and at times mistakes living children as her own.

The most daggering recollection I have of La Llorona is the time I spent a night at my father's house in Douglas, along with my then two small children. My father had gone to bed early that evening, falling asleep about the same time my children did. One was about three and the other five years old.

My father was asleep in his nearby bedroom and my children were each on a separate couch in the living room, while I was on the floor. One of my sisters was in a back bedroom. I could hear my father's light snoring and the gentle breaths of my children as they peacefully slept. A quiescent scene.

The night was unusually dark and quiet. I finally felt sleepy enough to turn the television off and cuddled up in my sleeping bag. Just as I was on the verge of drifting off into the first stages of sleep, I began to hear a cry in the distance. At first, I thought it was a dog, but then the sound came closer and louder. I heard my sister from her back bedroom say, "Francine, do you hear that?"

The distance cry turned into wailing and was quickly upon the house and before I could utter a word, my older sister was already entering the living room.

A depiction of the tormented ghost that searches for her children, whom she murdered. *Brittany Maklary.*

The horrible, eerie sound of the demonic banshee was so fantastically terrifying! It was a woman's voice and now her scream was coming in from a front open living room window. La Llorona was directly in front of me!

I could feel her demented energy pushing at the glass and I saw the figure of a head with long, white, flowing material that went from solid into a mist behind her. It was moving as if she was under water. She was looking into the house, searching.

My sister screamed, "Oh my God! Francine, go to her on that couch, I'll go to her! Mom used to say if La Llorona is near children, she will try to take them!" In a trembling voice, she continued, "She can't break the bond of a mother and her child though."

I scurried over to my older child and she over to my youngest, as she was her godmother. We sat as close to the children as we possibly could without waking them up as we listened to the blood curdling screams of the haunted mistress outside on the porch. The sounds of the cries traveled from one front window to the other on the other side of the porch. Her wailing grew louder with each dreadful second. My children, with the grace of God, never woke up despite the entity's ear cracking screams.

La Llorona suddenly moved to the back of the house and continued her wails and cries at the back door. My sister and I prayed The Lord's Prayer out loud. The sinister wraith returned to the front porch and went back to the first window where she started. We in turn, prayed even louder and harder, drowning her out.

Finally, after several minutes, her weeping tones traveled around to the other side of the house and faded down the alley, toward the backyard. Eventually, her voice was gone, along with her hellish energy.

HORSESHOE CAFÉ

There is one mainstay business in Benson that has the heart of the community and, quite frankly, Cochise County as well. This is the Horseshoe Café, which first opened in 1937. It was owned and run by Bostic and Mable Williams and was purchased for $495. It stayed in the family for generations but is now owned by Patricia Colombo, who bought it in 2010 along with her husband, Mike, who recently died in 2017. Patricia has continued to run the café and is proud to be part of the iconic Benson business; she also has a fantastic outlook for its continued success.

According to an official flyer furnished by Colombo, the Horseshoe Café began as a small diner the size of a railroad car. The structure was constructed in the 1940s. Many other businesses were run out of the building over the decades, such as a casino, a barbershop, a lawyer's office and a room and boarding service. In the late part of the 1940s, the upstairs was made into an apartment. The living area had three bedrooms, and there were two bathrooms with a small galley kitchen.

An interesting fact with the café involves Randy Tufts and Gary Tenen, the discoverers of the Kartchner Caverns State Park in the Whetstone Mountains. During 1974, the time the two were exploring the limestone hills at the eastern base of those mountains, they made the café a "secret hangout" and came in regularly. This living cave is ranked as one of the top ten caves in the world. I met the two men on media day, an event that was held during its grand opening, as I was a reporter for a local newspaper. That was a great experience.

The Horseshoe Café in Benson, Arizona. *Author's collection.*

A giant neon light shaped like a horseshoe inside the café, which covers almost the entire ceiling, is the longest continuously running neon light and has been there since the 1940s. There is also another neon light outside in the front of the building shaped into a horse's head.

There is a mural of horses inside that was painted by well-known cowboy artist Vern Parker. Another western-styled mural is on an exterior wall in front of the parking lot and was painted by a local artist named Larry Scott. The two murals were neglected for some time before members of the City of Benson's program called Clean and Beautiful stepped in. They asked Colombo if they could start a collection to secure funds for the restoration of the paintings. According to the Benson website, the mission of Benson Clean and Beautiful is to encourage pride and involvement of citizens in projects that beautify and enhance the physical and visual environment of the city. Enough funds were raised by the community, and local artist Doug Quarles restored both murals.

Colombo shared more history involving her restaurant during an interview and mentioned that the café was passed down from Mabel Williams to her daughter Irma Zedaker, who ran it until both her parents were gone. After Zedaker passed away, her daughter Lorene Whaley and her husband ran it for a while; later, other restaurateurs ran it for a few years. Patricia and her late husband bought it when the Horseshoe was closed, and in 2020, Colombo's daughter Kim relocated to Benson from Texas to assist with the business.

As far as any hauntings at the restaurant, Colombo said, "We do have a ghost here. It is Mabel. Upstairs used to be her living quarters, and after her husband passed, she ran the restaurant. She never left and is around."

The owner had a lot to share on her paranormal experiences, and her staff has seen many things as well. She said that one day, she and some of her servers were laughing and talking to customers when a strange thing happened. She said, "Nobody was around by the dishes. You see, we put the dirty dishes on the counter to be scrapped. Nobody was standing there, and all of sudden, there goes the dishes all over the floor!" She added, "We have white dishes, and apparently Mabel hated white dishes."

Colombo also noted that while she and another server were opening the restaurant one early morning, the cook called to say that his car broke down. Her husband told her that he was going to lock them in and go and pick him up. "We had a little light fan in the dining room, and the other person with me said she couldn't get the light on. I said, 'I'll give it a try,' and as I was walking past the door of the Palomino room, which is a door that does not

The door that was violently swung by the invisible hands of the resident ghost at the Horseshoe Café. *Author's collection.*

swing, it just opens and closes. I glanced over there, and it was swinging like crazy. We thought someone was in there, and we both grabbed a knife, steak knives!" She continued, "I thought, 'Who in the heck is in here?'"

The two women went around the corner and back into the galley, and as soon as they arrived, the door stopped swinging. Colombo said she related their experience to the other server who opens on other days, and the woman laughed and said, "Sure, Patty." Then the café owner said the same thing happened to her.

The Horseshoe Café has cameras in different location of the building. Once, when Colombo's daughter was looking through camera footage, the café owner's granddaughter was standing behind her. Colombo commented, "My granddaughter said, 'What the heck is that, Mom?' My daughter's reply was that she didn't know. Upon more investigation, they saw that the camera caught orbs. We have tons of them. They are in the kitchen and look

The coffee maker, where several witnesses saw the coffee grounds basket leap from the machine, thrown by an invisible entity. *Author's collection.*

like they are where you would do the dishes or cooking. The orbs also travel to the dining rooms."

The owner concluded that it's as if the orbs are representing the ghost or ghosts that are haunting the establishment and are going through the motions of the chores of running a restaurant.

One of the more spooky and provocative supernatural actions for the café ghost involves a coffee maker and its coffee grounds. In front of customers and after a server put the coffee grounds in and the hot water had run through it, suddenly the entire filter basket and coffee grounds flew out of the coffee maker! Colombo wasn't there at the time but was told about it.

"I said, 'No way! How could that do that?' It must be from fatigue, so I asked for a new coffee maker. We thought, 'Maybe the metal is fatigued,'" commented Colombo. She added, "What happens next and makes a liar out of me? I had walked by the coffee machine, and just as I passed it, the coffee grounds [flew] out again!" She said that the customers who were sitting at the counter in front of the coffee maker were shocked. Colombo stated, "The grinds were hot too. That incident made me a believer!"

More paranormal activity involves the kitchen. A cook said that he had just set up at opening time when a pot suddenly fell. He didn't think much of it and put it back to where it was. Then, without reason, the spoons used for the soups started to fly around the room.

Mabel's ghost is likely the inspiration behind the paranormal activity that takes place at the café. She lived upstairs in the apartment with her dog. Her home was completely changed after her granddaughter Lorraine sold the building. The new owner made the area into a comedy club, and during a building inspection when Colombo was buying it, it was found out that a load-bearing beam was removed. Colombo did have that taken care of, but the dramatic changes most likely upset Mabel and disturbed her peace. Even though the old apartment is used solely as storage, Colombo said that a few of the servers will not go upstairs.

I was able to do a short ghost hunt after an afternoon rush at the café. Colombo took me upstairs to Mabel's apartment. It was humid and hot up there, as it was the end of July when I visited. The interior walls are gone, but you can see where each room was located, as the flooring for each room is still separated.

As Colombo and I stood in what was once the living room, we simultaneously felt chills and got goosebumps. At that point, I began an EVP session using my phone. Colombo said, "I have never felt anything like that up here!" During the recording, I asked if this was Mabel. Our

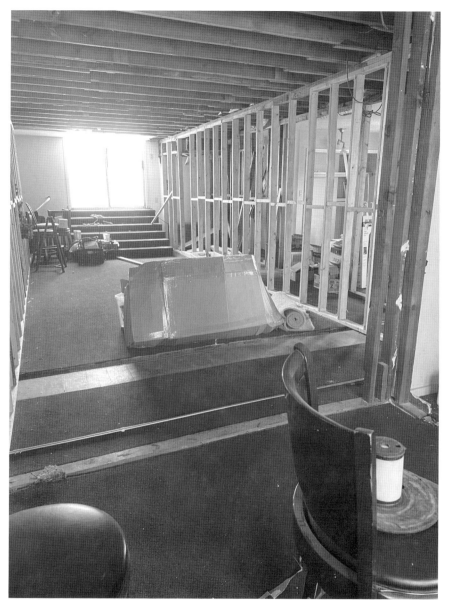

What used to be Mabel's apartment, where her voice was captured during a short EVP session. *Author's collection.*

goosebumps continued for several minutes. I felt them across my back and arms. Colombo expressed the same to me and repeated that she had never felt this before. She said she felt just chills. As she said this, I noticed that she was showing perspiration on her forehead from the heat of the room, but at the same time she was feeling chills. During an Arizona summer, it was strange to feel the chills up and down my body. But it was a reaction to the entity presenting itself.

I felt as if Mabel were sitting in a chair, positioned in front of myself, and asked if she was there. As I continued to speak, I heard a sudden noise near us. As the two of us spoke, and only after a few moments, we began to feel the chills come back and then dissipate again. This continued for a while. Colombo said that as many times as she had been up there, this type of experience had never happened to her.

We were standing in what was once the part of the living room. Colombo began to give a short tour of what each space was at one time—bedroom, kitchen and so on. As we walked around, I felt as if Mabel was following me. I asked the ghost if I could enter the bedroom area, and then she brushed right past me. I felt the cold air and nudge as she quickly went by me. After a few seconds, Colombo added, "Oh! She rushed right by me!"

Once more the goosebumps came back but in a stronger fashion. Colombo and I were amazed at was happening. I said, "Beautiful! Thank you for showing up, Mabel!"

The café owner mentioned that someone had seen a figure peering around a lone file cabinet left in the center of a room, near to what used to be the living room. Colombo added that noises were heard coming from the entity, but no one could understand the words it was saying.

After a bit, I realized that Mabel's paranormal activity had calmed down. I said in the recording, "Okay, I'm going to shut it off because everyone must go back to work. Bye, Mabel." You can hear Colombo gently laugh. Her voice is raspy, and after hearing mine in the recording, you could tell a difference in tones. We were the only people in the old apartment. At the very last second of the recording, right before I hit the stop button, there is a disembodied woman's voice that did not belong to either of us clearly saying, "Bye."

Mabel's death certificate states that she was born in Bisbee in 1895 and had lived in Benson for twenty-two years at the time of her death. She was in a one-car accident on Naco Highway just outside Naco, Arizona, on April 29, 1968. Her cause of death was due to multiple internal injuries, and she was transferred to Tucson Medical Center, where she arrived DOA. The death certificate lists her at seventy-two years of age, and she was buried in Tucson.

TRIANGLE T GUEST RANCH

Several years ago, I and a group of other ghost enthusiasts had the great opportunity to do a paranormal investigation at the Triangle T Guest Ranch, which is the second-oldest ranch in Arizona and sits in the Dragoon Mountains and the Cochise Stronghold. I wrote about it in my online magazine, *Spirits of Cochise County*. Following is the article in its entirety.

The ranch sits on sacred Native American ground, a place where the Chiricahua Mountain Apache chief Cochise would come for religious ceremonies. In the days before the pioneers and settlers, his group was the last Chiricahua Mountain Apaches to use the spot. The 160-acre ranch is located sixty miles southeast of Tucson and is in Texas Canyon. This area is stunning, with colossal boulders piled in curious formations surrounded by a southwest backdrop that is unmistakably Cochise County. The ranch celebrated one hundred years in 2022.

Linda Kelly is the owner of the guest ranch, and I interviewed her for my online magazine. She said that when the monsoon water flows off the rock formations that surround the property, they seem to give off an ancient energy.

In the 1800s, Kelly said that the Adams, a Texas family who were on their way to the California gold rush, broke down in the canyon and loved it so much they decided to settle there. They named it Texas Canyon and still own the ranch next to the Triangle T.

"In 1922, the owner at the time made a promise of marriage. He breached that contract, and as a settlement, the woman was given this ranch," stated Kelly. She added that Catherine Tuff became the new owner and was the one who made it a guest ranch. Kelly said that Tuff must have been of higher society, as her guest at the time included socialites like General John J. Pershing, the Vanderbilts and the Rockefellers. She added, "John F. Kennedy stayed here before he became president. The Kennedy family also stayed at the ranch. It was a good getaway for them in the mountains, so they could just relax."

There is a lot more history tied to the ranch in the Dragoons. During World War II, around the time of the bombing of Pearl Harbor, a Benson man named Reed Robinson heard a knock on his front door. He was told that he would join the military immediately and had to be ready in twenty minutes to leave, as he was going on a secret mission.

"His mission was to go to Honolulu and be part of the escort that brought two Japanese ambassadors and a spy back here to the ranch. They went

A stagecoach at the Triangle T Guest Ranch, where reports of ghostly figures have been seen and where psychic children said they felt negative energy. *Author's collection.*

through various train rides to make sure that they were not being followed. President Roosevelt had ordered for the ambassadors and their whole entourage to be brought here," stated Kelly. She added, "This place was rather unknown and obscure. They needed it to be very top secret because of the sensitivity they had toward the Japanese at that time. This is where they were held until they were later shipped out to be exchanged for some of our high-end officials."

In later years, the Triple T became a guest ranch again. The guest ranch has been a filming location for television and movies. Kelly said that many early western movies were filmed on the ranch, including the original *3:10 to Yuma*, *Tombstone* and *Geronimo*. The area has also served as the location for the television TV series *Young Guns*. Some of the movie stars who have visited the ranch include Clark Gable, Kenny Rogers, John Wayne, Glen Ford, Gregory Peck and Van Heflin.

The main house burned down several years ago, and the owners at the time did not think that another house was needed. They did feel that a saloon was a necessity for the guest ranch though. They built the saloon around a huge boulder that now sits in the middle of the actual bar. The saloon is called The Rock. The boulder used to be in the patio of the home. The house was where the pool is now.

"When I had my open house as the new owner, there were a lot of people who attended that used to work here for years. There was a woman who used to work in the dining room and said to me, 'Well, have you seen them?' I said, 'Seen who?' She answered, '*Them*.' 'Well, I see and meet a lot of people. Who are you talking about?' She answered, 'The spirits.'"

The guest of the open house celebration described the ghost she had seen to Kelly. She told Kelly that she saw a pioneer woman in the upper dining room and explained that she used to clean in there and would be careful that everything was put away. When she would come back into the dining room to check once more, there was always a place setting at the end of the table. She would just shrug that off, as maybe she forgot it, and then put it away. She would walk out and return, only to find it out again.

Kelly said, "This would happen on multiple times on different occasions. One night she said, 'Look, if you're going to do this, at least let me see who you are.' She then could see a wispy figure with a long dark skirt and a white blouse and a double bun put up and back." She added, "The figure just stood there and then vanished. That same description has been given to me by several people, including some of my staff. Our dishwasher has seen her standing at the kitchen door from the dining room looking at him." The upper dining room is directly off the kitchen.

The ranch owner said that she doesn't think the ghost is harmful—maybe a little mischievous at times. The ranch chef had put a bunch of pens on a kitchen counter, and when he came back, the pens were positioned in a starburst shape.

Kelly said that in the upper dining room, the table and the chairs, with the holes in the backs, are all original to the ranch, as is the buffet next to the table. The dining room is where I was able to capture an orb in a photograph. The closet in the dining room has only one light switch, which is also inside the closet. Witnesses have seen the light go on while the door is closed. They claim to shut the light off and then, as they are walking away, the light comes back on.

A small group and I went to the upper dining room to do a paranormal investigation of the pioneer ghost. As soon as our team and Kelly entered the room, half of us felt a cool rush of air beginning to surround us. We sat down with the lights off and began to do an EVP recording session. Several questions were asked out loud to the pioneer spirit. I asked the ghost if she was a maid there and to tap twice for yes and tap once for no. After waiting several seconds, a loud tap sounded.

Karla Jensen Rothrock, who was a part of our group, went into the kitchen and took pictures. After sitting in the doorway between the dining room and kitchen, she said that she noticed the back light of the kitchen was on. She asked Kelly if the light went on automatically because it wasn't on when she was in there a few minutes before. Kelly inspected and said that there are no automatic lights and that this may be a sign from the female ghost.

I had a personal experience during the EVP questions. As I sat at the table, I suddenly felt the chair to my left tremble. At the same moment, a very cold blast of air pressed against my back. This frigid touch stayed behind me for several minutes. The back of my shirt and pants were cold to the touch, but the room was very humid and warm, making the cold sensation odd. At one time, Kelly came behind me and felt the cool air I was describing. At that time, a photo of an orb was taken near her side.

Jensen said that she felt extremely lightheaded and dizzy when she went into the woman's bathroom off the dining room. She said she could not stay in there for very long.

Another report of paranormal activity at the ranch comes from the lower dining room, adjacent to where the pioneer woman spirit has been seen. "In the lower dining room, people have seen three men playing cards with their whiskey bottles on the table. They are usually seen when people are closing up and when it's late in the evening," said Kelly. She also said that she does not think the pioneer woman and men interact with one another.

The A&E Network filmed on the ranch for the show *Psychic Kids: Children of the Paranormal*, along with renowned psychic, medium and spiritual counselor Chip Coffey. Kelly said that the crew and cast did not know anything about the ranch and were scheduled to go to another destination that fell through the morning she got a last-minute call.

"We did not give them any information. They saw the same spirits I mentioned. In the upper dining room, a child on the show ran into the pioneer woman in the bathroom. They kind of startled each other. The spirit moved passed Coffey's group and went to the far end windows of the room and peered out as if she was waiting for someone. She is a little timid and quiet." My group captured a photo of an orb in the same area in where the children bumped into the spirit.

Some of the children filming said they also felt a negative feeling in the lower dining room, coming from the chairs. A little boy on the program felt a man staring at him. Kelly also said that the same boy on the program did see figures at the stagecoach on the property, and the children said that they felt negative energy there as well.

The ranch owner walked us over to room number 1, where a spirit called Grandmother Owanee has been seen. We captured a photo of a white glowing orb, a golden glowing orb and two orbs outside of room number 1.

"We had a housekeeper who was over cleaning room number 1. She kept coming in and out, in and out of the room on a windy day. Some maintenance guys heard yelling through the wind. They looked over toward room 1 and wondered why the housekeeper was rolling around on the ground," stated Kelly. She added, "She told the men that something was holding her down! We had a person who was a dowser living here at the time. She went to the room, and through dowsing and asking questions, she found out that a tepee was where the room is now."

The dowser said that a Hohokam Indian woman who was an advisor to the chief was present there. It was the Indian woman's prayer time, and because the housekeeper was being very active, she was disturbing her. The ghost, out of frustration for being interrupted, held the housekeeper down.

"We call her Grandmother because the dowser determined she was an older woman and grandmother. I call her Grandmother Owanee because the dowser said there was no way we could pronounce her name in her native tongue. The name Owanee just came into my head, so that is what we call her. The dowser asked her if it was okay that we called her that. She chuckled, as it wasn't her name, but she liked it," said Kelly.

A staff member said the night before our investigation that a guest went to touch room number 1's door, and it flew all the way open. The ranch employee said that it is hard for that to happen, as you must manipulate the door handle and latch each time you open the door. She said to the guest, "She was welcoming you. She probably wanted to communicate with you. Either you're locked out and you cannot get in or there's no problem."

Kelly said, "Before the incident with the housekeeper and having the dowser here, we used to have the hardest time getting into number 1. We would try the key, and it just wouldn't open. Later, the dowser said that Grandmother just wanted us to ask permission. Now when we have guests, we say, 'Grandmother, can you let us in?'"

When our paranormal team went to room number 1, we had to wait a few seconds, as Kelly had trouble opening the door. After the ranch owner asked Grandmother to allow us in, the door unlocked. An EVP session was immediately started in this room. This time, a pendulum was used. This instrument is an object hanging from a cord and used for yes and no answers. The spirit is directed to give an answer for yes or no in two different swinging motions given by the person holding the instrument. It can be forward for yes or side to side for no.

Randy Powers, Jensen, Kelly and I were all present during this séance and EVP session. I asked in a series of questions if she was indeed a Hohokam woman and if she was an advisor to chiefs. She answered "Yes" to all those questions. Through the pendulum, the spirit said that she recognized Linda and was pleased with how she was treating the land and the ranch.

I asked Grandmother if she liked all of us in the room and if she wanted us to stay. She answered "Yes." She was asked if she realized that she had died. The pendulum only went in circles—no answer. I asked her if there were other Native American spirits on the ranch. She answered "Yes." She was also asked through another series of questions if the spirit of Cochise was there. She said he was, but not always. When we left the room, we all thanked the female spirit.

Next, we headed over to room number 8. Kelly said that a guest saw a full-bodied apparition in that room before. Jensen had a personal experience with the ghost. As we sat quietly in the room, Jensen said that something was touching her neck. She put her hair up in a ponytail to make sure that it wasn't her hair. She then moved from sitting on one bed to another. A few seconds passed and it happened again. She said that it felt like a little tickle and continued for several seconds.

When Kelly was asked how she felt about all the reports of ghosts, she said, "I had so many reports of the same thing that I have to say there is something to them. I am not frightened here and have never been frightened on this ranch." She added, "I tell them [the ghosts], if they want to move on, go to the white light, but if they do not, they are welcome to stay here."

CARR HOUSE

There is a mystical place in the Huachuca Mountains where energy flows in and out of the forest and riverbeds. It's an essence of love and appreciation for those who choose to tell the history of the area and to never forget those who made this place home. This area includes a home called the Carr House, which sits in Carr Canyon in Hereford, Arizona. This interesting-looking structure was sold to the forest service in 1972 and was restored and ultimately turned into a visitor and information center by the Friends of the Huachuca Mountains (FOHM). This is a nonprofit organization that provides educational information of the history of that region. The center is located near the ruins of Carr Ranch, a pioneer community built by settlers around 1880.

The small group of pioneers who settled the area and lived there were from different generations and were creative people armed with a slew of various talents and loaded with ambition and a vision for a prosperous future. Carr House sits intact, but the ruins of Carr Ranch are now only crumbling retaining walls, falling fences and stairs leading to nowhere.

Let's start with the history of the ranch, which includes James (Jimmie) Carr, an Irish immigrant who was known as a "freight boss" and was one of the first in the region to start a freight business and construct the Huachuca Mill Toll Road with his sawmill at the top of it. Sawmills were in big demand in areas of boomtowns, and with Fort Huachuca nearby and with Tombstone growing, there was a dire need of lumber. The Gird/Carr (Carr Reef) sawmill was originally developed by Richard Gird, who saw the

The Carr House, located in the Huachuca Mountains, where there are reports of supernatural energies that blanket its existence. *Michael Foster.*

promising enterprise in the area. He bought the sawmill in San Francisco and shipped it by steamboat up the Colorado River to Fort Yuma. Then it traveled by wagons through Tucson and then to the Huachuca Mountains. It was up and running by 1879 and was bought by Carr in 1880.

Carr Canyon became the preferred title for the area. According to the book *Tearing Up the Ground with Splendid Results: Historic Mining on the Coronado National Forest*, Carr's sawmill produced 6,000 to 8,000 board feet of lumber per day. By June of his first year, it had produced an estimated 1,750,000 board feet, all done with a sixty-inch blade pushed by a twenty-four-horsepower steam engine. According to the *Tombstone Epitaph*, on March 1, 1887, Carr was expected to arrive home with sixty head of large Missouri mules. His mule teams transported ore from the two towns of Bisbee and Tombstone, charging $3.25 per ton. Only two years prior, the *Clifton Clarion* reported that in August 1885 he had purchased the entire herd of horses from H.C. Hooker of the Sierra Bonita Ranch. He bought the herd at $300 per head, totaling $37,000.

Carr was married to Ellen Tobin of the Tobin Seed Company from Kansas City; it was a long-distant relationship, as she moved back home after the birth of their son, Patrick. He eventually sold his toll road, 160 acres and sawmill business. After he sold more properties in other communities, he continued with his hauling business in the area of Mexico and the Southwest.

Another interesting individual connected there is a gentleman named Robert Todd, who made his way to Carr Ranch in 1887 after serving at

Fort Huachuca. According to a plaque at Carr Canyon, Todd built his home and put his focus on planting fruit, and when he filed for a homestead in 1909, he listed one thousand fruit trees. In 1898, he married a widow named Elizabeth Spence, an immigrant from England, and lived in Carr Canyon until he died in 1922. By 1925, Elizabeth had sold the ranch to her son and daughter, who sold it in 1929.

A veteran Civil War soldier named Charles Robert Biederman came to Carr Canyon in 1903. He was a German immigrant who joined General Tecumseh Sherman's band around 1860 and fought in North Carolina. He planted about three hundred walnut trees along Carr Creek and is also accredited with creating a method of grafting English walnuts to the native Arizona walnut trees. According to the FOHM website, Biederman was a horticulturist as well as an entomologist. One butterfly and three moths are named after him. Because of his accomplishments, he became a national treasure, and in March 1922, Arizona governor George W.P. Hunt came to Carr Canyon to visit with the "professor." Biederman died on June 23, 1932, from senile exhaustion at the Fort Huachuca Hospital.

Cicero Martin and Virginia Moson Martin built the Carr House in 1939 after moving from their Cerro Colorado Ranch in Mexico. Virginia is the daughter of Ella Roberts Greene, whose family was the owner of the OR Ranch, which housed their famous herd of cattle. Her stepfather was William C. Greene of the Greene Cattle Company in Arizona, the owner of the Cananea Cattle Company in the state of Sonora, Mexico.

Virginia's first husband was Ben Sneed, who worked as a cowhand for the family's cattle company and was an active shareholder as well. By 1911, Virginia was married to Cicero. Her new husband managed the family company from 1902 to 1959. The couple moved to their property, named the Two-Bar-L Ranch, in Sonoita, Arizona, in 1942, and Virginia died in 1963.

Another couple, named John and Ila Healy, lived at Carr Ranch from 1936 to 1972. John retired from the U.S. Army as a lieutenant colonel and fought in both world wars. He was stationed with the Tenth Cavalry in 1919 in Nogales, did a stint in the Philippines and retired at Fort Huachuca in 1935. The lieutenant colonel was the post school officer at Fort Huachuca, was involved with the Douglas Rodeo Association and was director of the annual spring horse show in Sonoita. The horseman/cattleman was also the chairman of the John Swain Memorial Fund, as well as other charities in the region. He is also noted as an author of various articles regarding his time with the cavalry and also diligently worked on the preservation of the buildings at Fort Huachuca. He assisted in the development of the Fort Huachuca Museum, which opened in 1960. Lieutenant Colonel Healy was born in 1891 and died in 1970.

Ila Harrison Healy had an interesting family lineage. Besides being the niece of Arizona senator James A. Harrison, she was also the descendant of two U.S. presidents: William Henry Harrison and her cousin Benjamin Harrison. Let's not forget that she was also related to Richard Morgan Harrison, who was one of the founders of the University of Arizona. Ila had nine siblings, and her father worked for the Duquesne Mines and lived in the Patagonia Mountains. Ila was an avid hunter, an ornithologist, a herpetologist, a lecturer and a writer. She hauled ore from Lochiel, Arizona, in her younger years and after she married John in 1920. She was the fort's trainer for the polo ponies and also was the polo team manager for the post. The couple ran a guest ranch on their property during the winter, and from May to October, they used it for asthmatic children. Ila was born in 1900 and died in 1985.

The Carr House is now open seasonally. The records of the Carr House and ranch are shared through photos, exhibits and wonderful story telling. Rosemary Snapp has taken the position of historian of the home and for the people who lived there. Alongside her is Mike Foster, the interpretive host, who has a flurry of information regarding the area as well as the property. I was able to interview them both before they closed for the winter season.

Foster said that during his time working there, he has the opportunity to speak with many people who have come to visit and recall numerous events that took place there, such as weddings and funerals; one person even claimed to have been conceived at the historical home.

During the autumn, Snapp and Foster set up a Day of the Dead altar to represent the people who lived at the house or even just visited. Snapp told me that her husband, Ralph, died in November 2020 and was now honored on the altar. Foster said that an unknown woman left a photo of a loved one for the celebration. "We still honor him and have set the photo there for the last three or four years," he said.

The staff here are striving to create a welcoming atmosphere for visitors, making an environment full of positive vibes and pleasant energy. This is true during the daylight hours, but Foster recalled a supernatural event that has stayed with him. He said that because of a flood during the monsoon season, he was forced to stay the night at the house. He tried to fall asleep, but between the lightning flashes, rain and the extreme eeriness of the house, he was forced to go to his truck and spend the night there instead. He said that he will not stay there overnight if he can help it.

"Sometimes no visitors come, and I am there alone in the house. I have been working there for the last nine years. About twice in these situations, I have felt an overwhelming eerie presence like someone was over my shoulder. After closing the blinds, I had to get out of the house as soon as I could." Foster told me that a past camp host named Geronimo (aka Jerry) had said that while at the Carr House, a dark or black orb seemingly stayed at his shoulder and followed him around the building.

Foster also said that a Yaqui man had recently visited the Carr House and asked him an eerie question. He stated, "We were in the big room with the fireplace, and out of the blue, he asked me if someone had died there. I asked him why he asked, and he said he could feel a heaviness. Then he went over and put his hands near the fireplace and said he could feel it there."

Snapp said that during her research, she found that a young boy had died in the house due to a brain aneurysm but doesn't recall anyone else. Both Foster and Snapp also told me that behind the Carr House there is a natural waterfall that has an incredible history of deaths attached to it. There have been about nineteen people who fell off the cliff in shocking and traumatic ways. Adults and children have perished there.

Carr Canyon Waterfall is eerily alluring and is historically the site where nearly twenty lives were cut short. *Michael Foster.*

There is a barrier blocking the area, keeping people from stepping close to the edge, but regardless of that, people young and old still climb over. There is a sign near the top of the waterfall and near the fence that people go through to reach it. It reads, "Dangerous Area. Keep out. Many lives have been lost by moving too close to the sheer drop behind this sign or sliding down the slick stream and over the falls. Stay Away."

THE COCHISE HOTEL

The town of Cochise, Arizona, has a significant and interesting place in the state's history. In 1880, this community was created around the Southern Pacific Railroad, which strung across what is now Cochise County. Train stations were placed at regular intervals across the rail line, including the one that started this town, which was constructed at Croton Spring Road and was named after the infamous Apache named Cochise.

The Cochise Station was small and only had a few train cars that were also used as employee housing. About four years after the Cochise Station was created, a man named John J. Rath arrived in the area. He worked as a night telegraph operator at Fort Bowie. He was hired as the railroad agent, and according to historical documents, he found water and dug a well and then persuaded the higher-ups at Southern Pacific to build a proper railroad depot. Rath was ambitious and was said to not only supply Cochise with water from his own irrigation system but also branch his system to supply the railroad with his water. Soon after the executives were convinced, the town of Cochise was created and considered a major shipping hub.

The twenty-eight-year-old Cochise founding father bought 120 acres at $1.25 each in 1896. He later surveyed that property and sold it as the land where the town was to be built. Once the depot was constructed, Cochise started to expand into a thriving community. It was a perfect spot for ore to be shipped out to Pearce, Arizona, and several other communities and mines in the area. In fact, a sixteen-mile road was constructed from Pearce to Cochise.

The Cochise Hotel. *Phillip Gessert.*

Twenty-four-horse freight wagons, full of ore, would travel from various mines on that road to put on trains heading to various smelters. Cattle was a big shipment at the station as well. There used to be cattle pens at the depot, as it is in the Sulphur Springs Valley, which was a thriving cattle country. The shipping depot also became a commuter station. On October 19, 1897, the Southern Pacific's new passenger train made its first stop there.

The Hotel Rath, built in 1897, was later renamed the Cochise Royal Hotel and Water Works. It has been a vital asset to the town of Cochise since its time of existence. Today, it is called the Cochise Hotel and is owned and run by a western historian and author named Phillip Gessert. I interviewed him, and he said that the hotel building was constructed by Rath and created with a post office and an express office. He also said that Rath served as the railroad agent as well as the Wells Fargo agent, justice of the peace and postmaster at a salary of fifty-eight dollars per year.

According to Gessert, Rath was a great businessman and partnered with Henderson's Saloon and, separately, owned the town's mercantile. The town's founder is also credited with starting a school district and being one of the members of its school board. There were other businesses in town, such as a restaurant, saloon, meat market and gambling hall.

In 1896, the young entrepreneur found time in his busy life to marry Lulu B. Olney. The couple eventually had three children together. They had some interesting guests and people who stayed or worked at the hotel in the years they owned and ran it. Gessert said that in 1899, a woman named Mary Katheryn Cummings was hired as a housekeeper at the hotel. History knows her as "Big Nose" Kate from her days with the infamous Doc Holliday and the Earps in Tombstone.

Arizona's first governor, George Hunt, while on a motor parade through the southern part of Arizona, picnicked in nearby Texas Canyon and stayed the night. Buffalo Bill's Wild West show came through, and even the Ringling Bros. circus performers stayed at the Cochise Hotel. Warren, Virgil and Wyatt Earp also checked in. In its heyday, the establishment served travelers, miners and others who were passing through and living in nearby towns such as Gleeson, Russellville, Courtland and, of course, Pearce.

Rath's town was a success, and it seemed like life was at a high point for the innovator. Sadly, on September 7, 1905, Rath came to his demise in a shocking accident. He and a group of his friends headed out for a hunting trip on a buckboard. Rath was sitting with a loaded shotgun next to him. The wagon hit some sort of rough spot, and his shotgun discharged, hitting him on the right side of his neck. He died instantly and was buried in his wife's family plot at the Desert Rest Cemetery.

"The hotel was owned by five different people throughout the years. I'm number five," stated Gessert. He bought the Cochise Hotel in 2013 and has a large collection of western antiques on display at the hotel from his forty years of working in the Hollywood film business.

I asked Gessert if he's had any paranormal experiences at his hotel. He said that many ghost hunters have investigated his building and have told them that ghosts are everywhere. He was also told that a previous owner is haunting the hotel. He said that the female spirit is in one of the exterior buildings and refuses to leave because she loves another male spirit that is haunting and watching Gessert. He also said that he was told a woman, who used to be a member of the tenderloin industry, is haunting the front bedrooms.

"Of course, everyone thinks it's haunted. Everyone that shows up and wants it to be haunted will see stuff," stated Gessert. He said that a large number of people have taken pictures and captured orbs in the photographs. "I have not really witnessed much, but I'm not much of a believer. But I do get a lot of people to investigate the hauntings. They never go away disappointed."

He also shared a story that includes a pair of mysterious slippers. "The strangest thing. We had a paranormal group coming in to visit. And suddenly in the middle of the road there was a pair of these slippers that looked like someone had just walked out of them. No one could figure it out," said Gessert. Apparently, as the group drove in, they saw them in front of the hotel. He said he thought that was weird and couldn't figure out why that happened.

Gessert said that the one of the previous owners had their child living with them in the hotel. The boy fell asleep on the floor in front of a heater in the parlor. The only other person in the building was the mother, but she was not in the same room. His hand was positioned directly under a rocker. The chair began to rock on its own and broke the boy's hand. The mother of the boy said that when he was explaining to her what had happened, he described a ghost woman in great detail. She said she didn't know who he was talking about.

There are more ghostly reports of guests hearing someone screaming for help, phantom sobs and footsteps up and down the main first-floor hallway when no one is there. People have also reported seeing a young girl appearing in the same corridor who then turns, runs down the hallway and dissipates. There is an antique spinning wheel that guests have seen turn on its own.

Gessert did say that something, perhaps of supernatural origin, has been bothering him over the years. He said, "My heating system in the hotel is a sophisticated electronic newer heating and air conditioning system. It is always getting messed with." He said that the temperature drops down or raises up, and he doesn't understand how it's happening. "That's the only thing I feel that is messing with me. It' mostly turns the heat up," he said. My response to him was that maybe the ghosts are cold. He replied, "Yea. Maybe."

CAMP NACO

THE BARRACKS OF THE BUFFALO SOLDIERS

On July 28, 1866, Congress created four all-Black regiments, also known as the Buffalo Soldiers; eventually, six regiments were established. Three of the units—the Ninth and Tenth Cavalries and Twenty-Fifth Infantry Regiment—were sequestered to Camp Naco, an army post located near Bisbee's city limits that is set about six hundred yards from the wall along the international border. They were sent there to enforce U.S. neutrality laws, maintain peace and to police the border.

The troops responded to border skirmishes as early as 1898, but troops reported to Naco for duty in November 1910, the same year as the Mexican Revolution. According to "Preserving Historic Camp Naco," a preliminary research report compiled by Debby Swartzwelder, the first battle of Naco, Sonora, occurred on May 19, 1911. Even though it occurred in Mexico, this event showed the United States that conflict along the border was inevitable. Vigilance would be necessary to protect U.S. interests.

The military post began as a large tent camp. The construction of the permanent compound consisting of twenty-three buildings began sometime between 1915 and 1917. The camp took up about thirty to forty acres of space based on references in quartermaster documents, but the lease of the property identifies the size as about ten acres.

The post has been called different things, but Camp Naco is the likely name of the compound during the time of the military's use of the area.

Camp Naco, once home of the Buffalo Soldiers, is now owned and being restored by the City of Bisbee. *Author's collection.*

Some refer to this site as Camp Newell or Newell's Camp, to honor John J. Newell, one of the original landowners of the Naco townsite and owner of the land where the camp is located. The property was leased to the U.S. government for one dollar, with the understanding that the land would be returned to the Newell family when the government no longer needed it.

Five thousand troops served at Camp Naco. According to "Buffalo Soldiers on the Southwest Border," an article by Helen Erickson, the soldiers were in age between twenty and fifty-two. They all met the requirement of being literate for enlistment, and they mostly came from the U.S. South. A Los Angeles newspaper reporter wrote in 1914 that forty-five men and women had been shot and killed by stray bullets along the border and near Camp Naco. In 1914, the Associated Press reported that Private Leroy Bradford, Troop B, Tenth Cavalry, was killed in Naco, Arizona, in a battle with Yaqui Indians. The camp closed in 1923.

The camp was used by the Civilian Conservation Corps in the mid-1930s, and the property also housed workers during the Depression. In 1990, VisionQuest, an organization that uses alternative treatments for juveniles in trouble, took up ownership of the property, with the intention to preserve the history of the Buffalo Soldiers.

Huachuca City, Arizona, a community located near Fort Huachuca, purchased the camp for one dollar from VisionQuest in 2006. This came about due to the organization not being able to get the correct zoning, as local citizens of Naco, Arizona, protested against the idea. As of 2018, the City of Bisbee had taken ownership of the camp with the guarantee to preserve the historical nature of the old army post. Bisbee also bought the property for one dollar. Friends of Camp Naco, the Naco Heritage Alliance Inc. and the City of Bisbee together strive to preserve the site's historic integrity while adapting the buildings of Camp Naco for future use.

On May 21, 2006, a fire destroyed several buildings of Camp Naco. In the past, the compound had been the victim of vandalism, and in 2013, while under the ownership of Huachuca City, grant money was obtained to get rid of asbestos found in the buildings and build a chain link fence around the camp to deter further damage and protect the public from any harm.

A paranormal investigation seemed to be the natural thing to do at Camp Naco. Our group, composed of five investigators, was let in through the locked gates to the camp by the late Huachuca City mayor, George Nerhan. We wandered the areas of the camp that were not off-limits.

To begin our investigation, we focused on the old hospital. Several photographs were taken as each person went through the empty rooms. We went to the rear of the building to begin our first EVP work of the night. Most of the questions—directed to any entity still bound to the building—were asked with the military in mind. I was recorded asking if any of the spirits were at the camp because of battles. A faint "yes" could be heard. When I asked if the entity was injured, an abrupt echoing "no" was heard from another area of the building. A few seconds after that, a clear but soft "no" was also recorded. At the same site of the EVP, a bright and luminous orb was photographed by Kenton Moore, who was part of our group.

We made our way to where the soldier barracks are located to the left of the hospital. Here we did more EVP work and used a pendulum as an instrument to communicate with any spirits lurking in the area. I read a list of questions designed for a Buffalo Soldier who had served at the camp to spark any memories he might retain. While Debe Branning, director of MVD GhostChasers, held the pendulum, I read information I had obtained from *Huachuca Illustrated* (volume 1, 1993).

I mentioned the names of Captain Herman Sievert, who commanded Troop A of the Ninth Cavalry in 1913, and Colonel William Brown, who led four troops of the Tenth Cavalry and arrived at Camp Naco in October 1914. I also read how crowds of visitors from Bisbee and Douglas came near the camp by carts, wagons and horseback to witness the battles. I mentioned that the soldiers arrived in Naco by the Southern Railroad. During one of the battles there, several gunshots had hit buildings; four troopers were wounded, and one horse and one mule were killed.

I asked if any spirit there knew that the Indians gave the soldiers the name "Buffalo Soldiers" and that the Germans called them "Hell Fighters." The pendulum began to swing "yes" to that question.

Branning asked the spirit if his bed was in the area where we were standing. He directed us to a space a few feet from where we were. We began to recite the alphabet and asked the spirit to tell us the first letter of his name. The pendulum finally swung "yes" for the letter *H*. Different names beginning with the letter *H* were mentioned, and the spirit finally said "yes" to the name Harry. We couldn't get an answer for his last name.

The questions continued, with Randy Powers asking "Harry" what troop had been barracked there. "Was it Alpha Troop?"

"Yes," was the answer.

"Was Charlie Troop next door?" Branning said that the spirit was getting excited due to the hard swinging of the pendulum to the answer "no."

Randy Powers asked Harry if his job was the troop guide on bearer, which is who carries the troop's pennant. The pendulum swung "no." After that, the pendulum began to slow down to any more questions—a sign that the spirit might be growing tired. Even though the spirit did not answer the last two questions, he did display an intelligent response to what his job may have been. A white glowing orb was photographed in the same building where Harry had communicated with us.

We left those barracks and continued to another set of living quarters located directly across from that building. Other photographs showing orbs were taken, but no other exceptional evidence was experienced.

This old military installation is a reminder of the great men who policed the border with honor and integrity. The Buffalo Soldiers are a large part of the U.S. Army's history and of Cochise County history. The continued restoration of Camp Naco and the future endeavors of its caretakers will highlight the men who lived there by showcasing their everyday lives and preserving their legacy.

BIBLIOGRAPHY

Arizona Capital Times. "The Bird Cage Theater." November 29, 2002.

Arizona County. azcounties.org.

Arizona Daily Star. "Historic Home." November 23, 2003.

Arizona Department of Health Services. "Elizabeth C. Swan Death Certificate." Arizona Genealogy Birth and Death Certificates.

Arizona Journal Miner. "Haldermans Hanged." November 16, 1899.

Arizona Republican. "Cold-Blooded Murder." April 10, 1899.

———. "ENTOMOLOGICAL Bulletin Blowflies, Grasshoppers, Crickets, Stinkbugs, ETC. ETC." July 17, 1905.

———. "Murders at Home." April 24, 1899.

Bisbee Daily Review. "Accident Victim Buys Auto." September 17, 1912.

———. "Bisbee Has Three-Quarter Million Fire Loss." October 15, 1908.

———. "Douglas Woman Dead from Morphine Poisoning by Her Own Hand." March 16, 1905.

———. "Feel from Train While in Tunnel." April 21, 1912.

———. "Funeral of Henry Marks." June 12, 1912.

———. "Man Killed in Crooks Tunnel." June 11, 1912.

———. "Roadmaster John Meets Quick Death." February 23, 1908.

———. "Train Goes in Ditch Near Crook's Tunnel." December 4, 1909.

———. "Tunnel May Open Today." June 6, 1905.

———. "Victim of Screw Worms." July 21, 1905.

———. "Warren School to Be Constructed on Most Moderen Lines." December 22, 1915.

———. "Woman Attempts Suicide at Douglas." March 15, 1905.

Bonaduce, Gretchen, owner, Greenway Manor. Interview, April 21, 2022.

Bradshaw, Patric, aide, Greenway Elementary. Interview, June 14, 2022.

Brekhus, Robin, owner, Avenue Hotel. Interview, June 13, 2022.

Cleere, Jan. "Western Women: Ila Healy Chased Lions, Snakes in the Huachuca Mountains." *Arizona Daily Star*, June 17, 2019.

Coconino Sun. "Brief News of the State." June 21, 1912.

Colombo, Patricia, owner, Horseshoe Café. Interview, June 24, 2022.

Copper Era. "Killed in Tunnel." June 28, 1912.

Copper Queen Library. "CQL Virtual Programs: Becky Orozco–Camp Naco." Bisbee, June 29, 2021. YouTube.

Curtis, Leslie, Arizona state park ranger. Interview, April 23, 2022.

Douglas Dispatch. "Gadsden Hotel Burns; Loss $200,000." February 8, 1928.

———. "Gadsden Was Opened in 1907 as One of Southwest's Best Hotels by Gadsden Company." February 8, 1928.

Farrell, Mary M., William B. Gillespie, Patricia M. Spoerl and John Peter Wilson. *Tearing Up the Ground with Splendid Results: Historic Mining on the Coronado National Forest.* 1995. Heritage Resources Management Report No. 15. USDA Forest Service, Southwestern Region.

Find a Grave. "Ila Harrison Healy." n.d. https://www.findagrave.com.

———. "LTC John Hillard Healy." n.d. https://www.findagrave.com.

Foster, Mike. "Carr Family." Vimeo, 2014. https://vimeo.com/93945389.

———. "Somewhere Beyond the Falls." Vimeo, 2018. https://vimeo.com/229035203.

———. "Spirit of the Carr House." Vimeo, 2007. https://vimeo.com/179825008.

Friends of the Huachuca Mountains. https://www.huachucamountains.org.

Geronimo. *Geronimo: The True Story of America's Most Ferocious Warrior.* Taken down and edited by S.M. Barrett. New York: Skyhorse Publishing, 2011.

Gessert, Phillip, owner, Cochise Hotel. Interview, June 13, 2022.

Gregor, Kay. "The Gadsden Hotel." *Cochise Quarterly* 3, no. 243 (Summer and Fall 1973).

Hames, Jacqueline M. "America's Haunted Army." U.S. Army, October 6, 2008. www.army.mil/article/13090/americas_united_army.

The Herald. "Heith's Hanging." Feburary 16, 1884.

Historic Pearce, Arizona. "Cochise." https://historicpearce.org/cochise.html.

Kellogg, Deren Earl. "Slavery Must Die: Radical Republicans and the Creation of the Arizona Territory." *Journal of Arizona History* 41, no. 3 (Autumn 2000): 267–88. https://www.jstor.org/stable/41696587.

Love, Robert, owner, O.K. Corral. Interview, August 4, 2022.

Maklary, Fran. *Mi Reina: Don't Be Afraid.* N.p.: PublishAmerica, 2004.

Marrero Publishing. "Cochise Origins." YouTube, October 15, 2015.

McNamee, Gregory. "Geronimo: Shanman, Seer and Warrior." *Natives People Magazine* (January/Febuary 2009).

Mohave County Miner. Mrs. H.H. Swan mention, July 5, 1905.

Porier, Shar. "These Walls Talk." *Herald Review*, March 4, 2007.

Powers, Francine. "Bisbee Fire Station No. 2." *Spirits of Cochise County*, 2009. spiritsofcochisecounty.com.

———. "The Bloodiest Cabin in Arizona." *Spirits of Cochise County*, 2009. spiritsofcochisecounty.com.

———. "Buffalo Soldiers at Camp Naco." *Spirits of Cochise County*, 2009. spiritsofcochisecounty.com.

———. *Haunted Bisbee.* Charleston, SC: The History Press, 2020.

———. "Haunted History: Bisbee Fire Station No. 2." *Bisbee Observer*, October 16, 2013.

———. "Triangle T Ranch." *Spirits of Cochise County*, August 2009. spiritsofcochisecounty.com.

Reuter News. "Ghosts Said to Mingle with Guests at Haunted Arizona Hotel." October 31, 2012.

Richmand Daily Dispatch. "Three American Citizens Murdered in Arizona by Peons." August 20, 1860.

Smith, Cornelius C., Jr. *Fort Huachuca: The Story of a Frontier Post.* N.p.: self-published, 1977.

Snapp, Mike Foster, and Rosemary Snapp, Carr House. Interview, November 24, 2021.

Sorensen, Wayne, Boothill Graveyard. Interview, April 15, 2022.

Southern Arizona Guide. "The Death of Chiricahua Chief Cochise, Part IV." n.d. https://southernarizonaguide.com.

———. "The Great Apache Chief, Cochise, Becomes 'Reservation Indian' to Save His People!" n.d. https://southernarizonaguide.com.

Tombstone Epitaph. "Yesterday's Tragedy." October 27, 1881.

Tombstone Nugget. "A Desperate Street Fight." October 1881.

Trischka, Carl. "A History of Cochise County, Arizona, Part II." *Cochise County Quarterly* 1, no. 2 (1971).

———. "A History of Cochise County, Part I." *Cochise County Quarterly* 1, no. 2 (1971).

U.S. Congressional Documents and Debates, 1774–1875. Library of Congress. https://memory.loc.gov/ammem/amlaw/lawhome.html.

Weekly Arizona Journal-Miner. "Terrible Condition of Mrs. Swan, Near Tucson." July 5, 1905.

Whetten, Bruce. "Douglas' Gadsden Hotel Under New Ownership." *Douglas Dispatch*, June 9, 2021.

Woolwine, Jeff, Haunted Encounter Adventures. Interview, May 3, 2022.

ABOUT THE AUTHOR

Francine Powers is an Arizona Newspaper Foundation award-winning reporter and a member of the Cochise County Historical Society. This paranormal historian has been on the television program *Ghost Hunters*, an online show named Streets of Fear on Fearnet.com, AzFamily 3TV from Phoenix and the *Tucson Morning Blend* show. She was also highlighted in the magazine *Vitality*, published by the *Sierra Vista/Bisbee Daily Review*, for her Bisbee Haunted Historical tour, which she owned and operated from 2013 to 2016. Additionally, she was the editor-in-chief of her own online paranormal magazine called *Spirits of Cochise County*. The online publication covered the history and reports of paranormal activity in southeastern Arizona. She is a Bisbee and Cochise County native and author of *Mi Reina: Don't Be Afraid* (2004), the first ghost book of its kind in Bisbee. She is also the author of *Haunted Bisbee*, which was adapted into a children's book called *Ghostly Tales of Bisbee*.

Photo by Brittany Maklary.